DATA, AI, AND NOISE

DATA, AI, AND NOISE

The Search for Truth in Information and Algorithms

DEREK W. GIBSON

WILEY

Published by John Wiley & Sons, Inc., Hoboken, New Jersey.

Library of Congress Control Number: 2026944167

ISBN 9781394424337 (Paperback)
ISBN 9781394424344 (ePub)
ISBN 9781394424351 (ePDF)

Cover Design: Wiley
Cover Image: IrhamAnifMaulana/stock.adobe.com. Generated with AI.

SKY10167825_090426

Contents

Introduction *ix*

1 The Information Apocalypse **1**

The Media Landscape—Decades in Decline 1

Communicating the Wisdom of Others 2

Libraries as a Source of Truth 4

Newspapers in America 7

To the Moon 9

The Internet (Obviously) 11

Trusted Institutions 14

Influencers, Your New Neighbors 15

The Noise of the Infodemic 20

2 The Negotiated Truth **23**

What the Newspapers Left Out 25

The Whole Story 27

When Truth Needs a Referee 29

What Is Truth? 31

Is the Moon Real? Is the Earth Flat? 33

To the Moon 36

A Simpler Explanation 38

Alternative Facts 40

Negotiating Truth 43

3	**Open Your Eyes**	**47**
	If You Can Dream It...	47
	Natural-Born Instincts	49
	Picture This	53
	I Do Recall	57
	Noise and Judgment	62
4	**Can a Computer Know Your Vulnerability?**	**67**
	Emotional Algorithms	67
	Concern or Legitimate Risk?	68
	Signals	70
	Personalization Engines	72
	Exploitation Mechanism	79
	The Scale Problem Solved	82
5	**When Certainty Fails**	**87**
	You Are Not Helpless, and Neither Is the Truth	87
	Anchors in an Ocean	90
	Embrace Uncertainty	91
	Source over Content	93
	Recognize the Noise	94
	Identifying the Rush	95
	Compensation and Incentives	98
	A Different Kind of Journalist	101
6	**Empowering You**	**107**
	The Verification Moment	107
	AI vs. AI: The Technology Arms Race	108
	How Detection Works	111
	Five Stages	113
	Steering the Algorithms	116
	Early Morning	117

7 You Are the Target **121**
The Digital Twin You Never Met 122
Finding Your Friends 123
Personalized Reality Machine 127
Invisible Feedback Loops 128
A Newsstand of Information 130
Data Ecosystem Beyond the Feed 131
A Different Worldview 134

8 Community and Collective Intelligence **139**
Our Shared Reality 139
The Limits of Centralized Control 142
Promise and Hope in Crowdsourced Verification 147
When Collective Intelligence Fails 154

9 Global Scramble for AI Rules **159**
The Brussels Effect 159
The Power of AI 160
Three Global Models, No Consensus 166
The Exploits of Regulation 170
Self-Regulation by Default 176

10 Living in the Noise **183**
In the Room 183
This Is Not Normal 187
The Weight of It All 189
Truth, Eventually 192

Acknowledgments *197*
About the Author *201*
Index *203*

Introduction

The clouds of smoke leapt into the air. Dark and sooty, they contrasted starkly with the morning blue sky, their edges rolling like boiling water, allowing glimpses of the flames at their base. It looked like a monster entrapped behind a row of crowd-containment fencing that contained it as it billowed in front of the Pentagon. The fencing, a useless security measure against an explosion that now created a column of smoke and fire several times higher than the building itself.

It was shortly after 9 a.m. on what was otherwise an uneventful Monday morning on May 22, 2023. For the staff at the Pentagon, this would be a terrifying reminder of dreadful events from many years before, when the building was struck during the 9/11 attacks. Wall Street quickly took notice, and the markets dipped—another attack shortly after the recent Russian invasion of Ukraine might mean something more to come. The United States' compassion for Ukraine was a complicating factor. For everyone else in America who saw the picture online from many news outlets, beginning with Bloomberg News, it created another type of terror.

It was the dread of misinformation fueled by a new type of technology—generative AI (GenAI).

In the hours that followed, people realized that it was not a *real* attack and that the image was contrived. Made with a purpose. However, it required an official statement posted by the Arlington,

Virginia Fire Department and further confirmation by a Pentagon spokesperson to assure some that this was not real.

The original post showed up on Twitter, which over the years had become increasingly a place where people got their news in near real time. Twitter was perfect for people who wanted to quickly consume information. With its limits on the size of posts, it offered seemingly endless tidbits of news interspersed with other entertaining items people had come to enjoy.

The post was not actually from Bloomberg *News*, but from an account masquerading as a legitimate news service named Bloomberg *Feed*. Subtle name differences go unnoticed in our fast-paced scrolling. This alternate account was not associated with the real Bloomberg organization; however, it was indeed a verified account with its noted blue checkmark. Verification provided authenticity.

At the time, Twitter made some changes to the process that people or organizations needed to follow to become verified following its acquisition by Elon Musk just a few months earlier. To be blue-checkmark verified required only a monthly subscription payment and two-factor authentication. Less than $10 and a phone. Ironically, the checkmark process that originally began as a way to keep impersonators and fraudsters away, now made it easier for them to come to the platform with branded credibility. Twitter users might not have been keeping up with the changes in obtaining a checkmark and were still accustomed to seeing it as a badge of trust. The stage for a new form of misinformation was coming together.

Another key element was the use of artificial intelligence, or AI. An important innovation was recently introduced, and in May of 2023 the world was just coming to know ChatGPT. It was the first popular large language model (LLM) from OpenAI introduced in the fall of 2022. Its introduction remains a marked moment in technology history that is comparable to the development of the personal computer (PC) or the Internet. Then again, six months after any new technology, how many people on Twitter even knew about it?

Technology innovations have had a profound impact on how people find information. The PC put the power of computing in the hands and homes of regular everyday people. Before then, they would have needed to be part of a large company or a university to get access to a computer—an exclusive club. As a descendant of the larger mainframe computers at those institutions, the PC, in its smaller format, empowered people. The Internet too was an enabler that connected people and information. With access to the Internet, nearly everything known or knowable could be gathered practically for free, or at least for less than the cost of a set of encyclopedias.[1]

ChatGPT was a similar innovation—a GenAI milestone. And soon, along with its competitors such as Claude, Copilot, and Gemini, it would be simply referred to as "AI." What had for decades been a term used to describe a broad use of data, statistics, scientific methodologies, and computers in a system to replicate human intelligence tasks, AI took on a new meaning. AI is now mostly associated with GPTs (generative pre-trained transformers) like ChatGPT. From a user's perspective, the wonder of the experience has been its conversational nature. This change in how we interact with computers also changes how we think about the information they provide. We tend to trust AI more, although there is less reason to do so, and briefly, as we feel like we are talking to a person, we suspend our skepticism about what it shares with us.

Back in 2023, there was another emerging technology using a similar process to ChatGPT, and that was all about creating pictures. From text-prompt-to-answer was now adding text-prompt-to-picture. Tools like Stable Diffusion, Midjourney, and OpenAI's very own DALL·E (a playful name combination of Spanish surrealist artist Salvador Dalí and the Disney-Pixar animated robot WALL-E) were the initial leaders in this space. They allowed people to type brief descriptions of pictures that they wanted to see, and in minutes these tools created them. From your imagination to reality. Perhaps a more impressive feature was that they could be edited, not with traditional photo-editing tools, but simply with words. Photo editors like Adobe Photoshop are expensive and difficult for a novice to use. In the hands of a skilled graphic designer, they are great, but they take time and skill to use properly. The GPT-like image creators lowered the talent threshold, and to drive early adoption, they were mostly free. Now, anyone with an idea and a short text description can create a picture of anything. Not just a pixelated computer image, but something that is virtually indistinguishable from a real photo.

So how do we know if something is real and where it came from? One approach is watermarks. Watermarks are an age-old technique to label something either as authentic or to identify its source. Their history dates to the 13th century in Italy, where the practice was first introduced. The watermark is named for the traditional process during the paper's manufacture, where adding water to a metal stamp thinned the paper with the image of that stamp. When held to the light, the image could be seen, and it was a common way to discourage counterfeiting. Similar practices carried on into the modern era, where more complex watermarks were added to postage stamps and paper currency. It is a short leap to conclude that as knowledge that was captured on paper is now digitized, so too would be the watermark, but digital watermarks have their limits, and one is the willingness of new technology to adopt them.

The race for AI dominance continues to rely on a lax approach to safety, and the early days of AI imagery were no different. When DALL·E, Midjourney, and Stable Diffusion introduced their tools, the digital "stamp" or watermark indicating that an image was created by AI was seemingly an afterthought, if it existed at all. Of these three tools, only DALL·E added a small icon to the bottom of a photo, although that could be easily cropped out with a simple editing tool.

Later, in 2024, when OpenAI introduced its *third* version of DALL·E, it joined the Content Authenticity Initiative and adopted the Coalition for Content Provenance and Authenticity (C2PA) standard. C2PA embeds data into images, video, text, or audio files that reveal when, where, and how they were created. It also tracks edit history if the file is manipulated. The protocol was created in early 2021 and began as an initiative led by Adobe, *The New York Times*, and Twitter. It was later joined by many other technology companies.

While digital watermarks are a great *idea* against misinformation, they require something most humans do not do. We do not typically pause to check the *provenance* (i.e., the watermark) of something we see online, especially when it is urgent and terrifying, like an explosion at the Pentagon. In other words, we do not act rationally to the information we see. What happens in our brain is a response that is hardwired into our DNA from an evolutionary survival mechanism. The emotional processing center of your brain is called the amygdala, and when it encounters a danger—as viewed online or in real life—its response is the same: it prepares your body for survival in the classic fight-or-flight response without any initiative from you. It is an automatic process that also shuts off the rational reasoning part of your brain in your cerebral cortex, which is the area that regulates voluntary actions like thinking and decision-making. You are now on autopilot.

With rational thinking suspended, the equivalent of yelling "fire!" in a crowded theater occurs; that is, we repost the online image to notify all of our friends. We must make sure everyone knows about this threat. Immediately! Fortunately, it is so easy to do, with social media platforms all having very clickable methods to reshare content. Some, like Meta, make it easy to share content across multiple apps such as Facebook and Instagram simultaneously.

It may not be rational, and if social media platforms were trying to help you stay calm and be logical in your thinking, they would not make it so easy for you to have these types of knee-jerk reactions. For the platforms, when we are acting emotionally, that just registers as better content. Psychologist Daniel Goleman termed this emotional overreaction *amygdala hijacking*, and it is built into the design of social media platforms. Would it not be better if, before reposting something online, we were required to click twice? Perhaps with an added message that says, "Are you absolutely sure you want to share this? And have you verified all of the sources?" Even better would be if the platform offered built-in links and resources to check the validity of the original content. Instead, we yell "fire!" and then calm our emotional responses, knowing we have done all we can to protect others.

At the same time that we are viewing our news on our social feeds, we give less thought to viewing the news from traditional sources. In the moments when people are seeing the picture of the Pentagon explosion, they are *not* seeing it on broadcast TV or online on the established media websites like *The Washington Post*, *The Wall Street Journal*, or *The New York Times*. Are they hearing the same news on public radio or from government sources? All of these traditional sources of information are not consulted because social media has morphed into an information-everything service. What began as a truly social experience, where people would chat and connect with friends and family, has become a marketplace and pseudo-information hub. People start their morning online chatting with friends and stay there throughout the day for everything else, including seeing what is going on in the world. For platform providers, this is exactly their goal: to keep people online as long as possible, to test your likes and dislikes, and to gather information that can be used to promote ads based on your data. And if that includes some news, or something news-adjacent, then even better.

■ ■ ■

The choreographed Pentagon explosion had all of the pieces in place to deceive with AI. The topic was familiar from the 9/11 attacks and likewise shocking. Given that an attack had happened before, the story immediately had credibility. It would be memorable enough that people doomscrolling would not pass it by. The placement on Twitter was where people now expected to see their news, conveniently customized by the algorithms. By 2023, 50% of US adults reported getting their news from social media.[2] At the time, there was an ongoing war that had started the year before between Russia and Ukraine. Another element of familiarity, it was often part of the daily news that the United States was providing military support. Support that was managed from that very Pentagon building. Topics of explosions and terror were relevant. They were real. This story fit a plausible narrative—the Pentagon could have been targeted with an explosive device. Surely it made sense. There were believable means and motives.

The rules of verified accounts on Twitter had changed, both making it easier for bad actors to be verified and encouraging everyday users to retain their assumptions about what verified really meant—a blue check mark on an account that looked similar to a trusted news organization still gave meaning: verified, authenticated, and trusted.

Then there was that picture. It was realistic due in part to its creation by AI. Long an expensive task with barriers of time, money, and talent, creating such an image was no challenge to someone who wanted to be deceptive. Type a description of the scene you want to create, and AI can generate it in a heartbeat. Ask AI to make the scene more dramatic or menacing, and it can do that too. As the director of a scene, people using AI do not need to work like graphic designers, who know what elements of a picture to change, like the contrast of the sky and smoke, to make it look more dreadful. They simply ask AI to make the picture more terrifying, and it is done.

Amateur artists in the hands of fearmongering opportunists have become fans of AI overnight.

The story and picture of the Pentagon explosion were not real, although they were among the first to be aided by AI. The GenAI capabilities of early 2023 were comparatively in their infant stage, just learning to walk and create and build. GenAI at its outset was notably thought of in a positive way. As tools, they would improve information searches and be a better tutor for the curious. Like many new technologies, we embrace what they can do and fawn over the potential for their future. We do not spend much time thinking about the bad possibilities, or how they could be used in negative and nefarious ways—our DNA is not hardwired to continuously think about bad outcomes.

The digital dust quickly settled after the Pentagon explosion story. Many rational-thinking people posted that it was not real. Others noted that they had just driven by the building and there was nothing there—no smoke, no fire, no emergency. Digital authenticity requiring in-person human verification had become real.

The stock markets readjusted. People scrolled onward to other things in their social media feeds. The Pentagon carried on as it always does. However, things were different. We had seen AI, its optimism shadowed by its use in a malicious way. The purpose was murky at best—a bad actor, a foreign government trying to cause disruption, or a prankster looking for a thrill? We may never know, which is among the many hidden consequences of AI. What we do not know.

In the chapters that follow, we will look at all these factors that are increasingly causing us to struggle to find the truth in the noise. We will explore the consequences of changes in our information ecosystem, with the rise of social media and the decline of establishment media, along with the contributing factors of deteriorating trust in authoritative information from governments and academic institutions. As a result, we collectively struggle to know where to look for the truth.

Information is coming at us in great volumes, and our non-digital-native brains are not well equipped to manage the modern era of AI overload. At the same time, the nature of AI systems also tends to leverage these primitive weaknesses. We must remain optimistic and recognize that AI also has tremendous power and is shaping our world in positive ways. However, the rate of change, its rapid deployment, and ever-changing capabilities raise concerns—those of missing guardrails and ambiguous and often disjointed policies and regulations. The influence AI will have on society will persist for decades, and it is best for all of us to know more about how AI works and how we can better manage this new world.

Let's begin.

Notes

1. Prior to the PC and the Internet, books were the primary source of information for research. Owning a set of encyclopedias, a vast collection of information captured in a series of hardbound books, was a true investment. The well-regarded Encyclopaedia Britannica sold for $1,200 in the 1960s, or the equivalent of $12,000 in today's dollars.
2. Pew Research Center, "Social Media and News Fact Sheet," www.pewresearch.org/journalism/fact-sheet/social-media-and-news-fact-sheet

DATA, AI, AND NOISE

Chapter 1

The Information Apocalypse

The Media Landscape—Decades in Decline

Before we begin to understand how AI is changing our media landscape, where and how we get trusted news and information, we must first understand how we gather information and communicate it with others. We need to identify how some parts of the information we find are important while others are discarded. This is our verification process, what we trust and what we do not, and it is as old as humanity.

Imagine you are transported back in time. It is the year 32,000 BCE, and you are standing in a cave. On the wall, you notice a drawing. The drawing, a pictograph, is an early form of written language. It depicts several men throwing spears at an animal. The animal has been cornered. In the background, there is a distinctive river drawn that you recognize as being nearby.

In this era, early humans were known to travel in small groups, moving from place to place, foraging for food. They would briefly settle in an area. When the food stocks ran low from depleting what they could gather from the land and hunt from the area, they would pick up and move on to the next place. What if they knew where to go next, where food and hunting animals were plentiful? They would have an advantage.

You stare again at the painting on the wall. You have only recently discovered this place, having never been to this area before. What is the meaning of the pictograph? What is the message? You look at it and conclude there are two things to be known. One, hunting in groups, as these men did, is more successful than hunting alone. Coordination, collaboration, and sharing tasks are beneficial to all. Two, this area, near the river, is where there are the most animals to hunt. It is fertile land, and perhaps the animals are here, everywhere in abundance, drawn to the edges of the water where they may be vulnerable. This makes sense. The message is clear: stay here, hunt here, no need to go anywhere else. Do you believe it?

As a young cave dweller with your group depending on you, you now find yourself confronted with possible misinformation.

When we encounter new information, we tend to first *see what we want to see*. If it benefits us, we trust it. This is our confirmation bias in action. But what if we want to validate our conclusions? We might rely on our community, our friends, and neighbors—the other members of our tribe might have experience and can provide insights. Good knowledge is kept. The rest should be tossed away. The experience and wisdom of others can be passed orally or written in some form, just like the painting on the wall.

Trust the wall.

Communicating the Wisdom of Others

Early humans benefited from that community and the wisdom of others who shared knowledge by retelling stories. Those stories could have been about how best to hunt or how to avoid dangerous animals and situations. Human language dates back at least 100,000 years. Although the timing of its origins is debated based on the fossil record, one thing that is agreed upon is that human language requires trust. This differs from other animals, including primates, that are less trustful of their peers.

In humans, trust is a foundation of creating community and conveying ideas that are not immediately present. Animals instead rely on sounds and gestures that are dependable and hard to fake. What they can touch, see, and feel is very real, and everything else might just as well not exist for them. Humans, however, by trusting other humans, can agree on the structure, grammar, and rules of language. They can express metaphors and more complex concepts like names of numbers, money, and the idea of a corporation as an entity. These concepts only really exist because of trust in a particular idea: a corporation has been incorporated; therefore, it exists if we *all agree* it exists. Corporations are not tangible, yet in our society we treat them almost as if they were a type of person. Community and shared common goals helped create language because of trust. As a result, we tend to give away our trust. It is part of who we are.

As civilization began to conform to these ideas of trust and shared knowledge through language, there was eventually a need for written language too. Oral traditions through storytelling have limited capacities. Written language dates to about 3,500 BCE and the Sumer region of Mesopotamia, which used clay cuneiforms. Around 3,200 BCE, Egyptians began using hieroglyphs. Cuneiforms and hieroglyphs were both forms of writing using pictures to convey stories. The Phoenicians developed an early form of written language around 1,900 BCE that was later modified by the Greeks.

The Greeks added vowels and changed the direction of reading to be left to right. With some later minor additions of symbols by the Romans, this became the basis of our current alphabet used in most Western languages. Independently, around 1,200 BCE, China began developing its written language, demonstrating that as societies evolved, humans required a written language to share knowledge. Without writing, knowledge of everything from the best way to plant and harvest crops to the value of hunting in groups was shared as a story.

The most famous orally shared stories that were later committed to written form were the poems of the *Iliad* and *Odyssey*. Each was attributed to Homer as the author, although given the long time and repetition of the stories, it is more likely that there were many contributors. The genesis of each story dates from the Late Bronze Age and preserved real memories of the Mycenaean civilization circa 1,200 BCE. This was the period of the Trojan War, and they served to provide the foundations of a shared Greek culture. Every good sustainable society needs to nurture its culture. The stories of war, of sacrifice, loss, and heroes helped establish their culture and shared experiences that bond individuals into communities. The poems helped establish ethical and moral expectations and guided trust in each other.

More than 500 years from the genesis of the *Iliad* and *Odyssey*, these stories, each about 140,000 words, became written manuscripts. They were copied and rewritten over time with changes along the way. Perhaps an accidental edit, a word inserted, or a meaning changed. Until they were codified with the invention of the printing press in 1436, people could change parts to suit their needs. The truth of the manuscript was malleable.[1]

Over time, shared knowledge became truth. When something is written, it can be referenced. It can be verified, and this was an important moment in building trust within societies.

Libraries as a Source of Truth

The 2021 novel, *Cloud Cuckoo Land* by Anthony Doerr, tells a story of multiple timelines that centers around a fragmented ancient Greek codex of the same name. Similar to modern bound books, a codex was a stack of written pages, usually made of vellum or parchment, that were bound together. The format replaced long winding scrolls used during the Roman Empire.

One of Doerr's storylines includes the characters salvaging books from a library before they are destroyed in 1453 during the Siege of Constantinople. The premise of this storyline is about the fact that through time many ancient books of literature have been lost to natural disasters, war, or neglect.

The most famous of these lost libraries is the Library of Alexandria, which was established in Egypt circa 283 BCE. It was created by Ptolemy I, who succeeded Alexander the Great. The library was a tremendous scholarly resource containing hundreds of thousands of books and scrolls from Greece, Egypt, Persia, and India. The library established a center of learning and a symbol of an intellectually superior society. With works of literature, history, law, mathematics, and science, it attracted the scholars of the day from around the Mediterranean, who lived, researched, and studied on site. Individuals included Strabo, Euclid, and Archimedes.

With knowledge comes power and prestige, along with the envy of your enemies. The struggle for power was also a struggle to control information. As a result, the library came to a tragic end when it was destroyed by fire during a battle between the Roman ruler Julius Caesar and the Egyptian rulers in 48 BCE.

The Imperial Library of Constantinople was another example of empires building libraries. Following the demise of the Roman Empire, the Byzantine Empire under the leadership of Constantine the Great established this library in the fourth century CE. It grew to contain an estimated 120,000 scrolls.

What did ancient empires teach us about the importance of written books? What do these societies, more known for their military innovations and conquests of land, have to do with libraries? The books, the libraries, and the scholars they attracted became the engineers, inventors, and truth-tellers of their time. They invented both medicine and military machines superior to those of their enemies. They created poetry and stories that bound together people in society. A shared history and common experience connect the heart and soul.

Leaders who could convince their populace with words rather than physical coercion or suppression were more efficient and successful. As they fostered written books, they also fostered places of authority and dependable institutions of information. Knowledge, it seems, really was power of a less lethal form. It could be wielded to move a nation, and once the kings, emperors, and sultans learned this, their desire for creating and controlling libraries grew.

Modern libraries had this same type of empowerment for people, especially when society became more literate. In the ancient era of the Library of Alexandria, the people that could read were limited to scholars, priests, and government officials, perhaps 10–15% of the population.

Things began to change in 1436 when Gutenberg invented the printing press. The number of written books rapidly increased. With more books and more readers, libraries became more useful to other people beyond the officials of society. The literacy rate in Europe at the time was 30%, but as books became more abundant and affordable, literacy rates rose. By 1696, the literacy rate in England grew to 47%.

By the time young colonial America arrived, people were thirsty for knowledge, especially about philosophy and law, and new ideas on government. The literacy rates in parts of America were higher at 90%. While this varied by region, there was at least a growing appreciation for the written word and the knowledge it provided.

Books were still relatively expensive to own, so Benjamin Franklin established the Library Company of Philadelphia in 1731 as the first public-lending library.[2] A library of this kind allowed subscribers to borrow books for a small collateral payment and return them when they were finished reading. In the early days of the new US government, the Library Company of Philadelphia served as a predecessor to the Library of Congress by providing access to lawmakers. It still exists and remains open to the public.

While libraries provided references to known facts of history, science, and laws, they were not a good resource for providing updates on everyday events. For this, people relied on newsletters, which eventually turned into newspapers.

Newspapers in America

The first regularly published newspaper in the United States was the *Boston News-Letter*, beginning in 1704 in colonial Massachusetts. Many of the early newspapers were about politics, and soon they evolved to provide other news topics. Soon newspapers with names like the *Patriot Press*, *New Jersey Journal*, *Harfort Courant*, and *Pennsylvania Gazette* were common weekly publications. In 1783, the *Pennsylvania Evening Post* became the first daily newspaper. The American Revolution created interest in history and law and helped spawn the great American democracy experiment. In the brief following years, it created an appetite for news of its progress.

Newspapers grew in popularity along with the United States Postal Service, which offered favorable rates for their distribution. As the number of post offices grew, so did the number of newspapers. The Post Office Act of 1792, signed by President George Washington, created the framework for the distribution of information both as person-to-person letters and as newspapers. It authorized Congress to create a distribution network of roads and established privacy rules against unauthorized opening of mail, thus promoting the free flow of information.

Initially in the Northeast and then westward through the Ohio Valley, as the nation migrated so did its news. In 1790, there were 73 post offices and 96 regular newspapers. By 1830, there were 8,450 post offices and 861 newspapers. A total of 16 million newspapers were delivered in 1830 at a time when the population was 12.8 million.[3] In the days before the Civil War, a trip to the post office was more than an administrative task; it was how people communicated, gathered knowledge, and perhaps heard a rumor or two.

Newspapers of this era were geared toward the aristocrats of the time who were focused on business and the rapid changes brought upon by the Industrial Revolution. This new type of revolution was changing industries around the globe, and in the United States, it landed squarely on the shoulders of the working class, who were faced with changing jobs and skills because of rapid technological changes. For many of them, access to subscription libraries and newspapers costing six cents was limited. The concept of public education and common schools that could supplement their education was still in development in the 1830s.

The working class, whose literacy rates were increasing, felt disenfranchised and left out at a time when the United States was in the throes of change—a pattern that would repeat in the future.

While workers were looking for a voice in the newspapers, the Industrial Revolution also changed business models from small independent handcrafters to large commercial operators. Those organizations had a need to market their products broadly both geographically and to a wider socioeconomic audience. To do this, they needed a different type of newspaper, one with mass appeal.

In the fall of 1833, Benjamin Henry Day launched *The New York Sun* to fill this need and, in doing so, created a new type of journalism. His newspaper was priced at just a penny and sparked what would be known as the beginning of the Penny Press Era. Its format was smaller, with fewer pages, yet its style, which invoked the interest of the "common man," was quickly popular. Its success prompted many others to replicate this type of populist publishing. The paper featured more advertising, less politics, and more about jobs, including a sizable Help Wanted section. This appealed to the working class unlike any other previous publication. To garner distribution, they created the practice of paperboys, who would sell papers on the city's busy corners while sharing highlights of the news to passersby. It became a top-selling newspaper.

To the Moon

By 1835, *The New York Sun* was a prosperous newspaper, although it was facing growing competition from the other penny papers. They wanted to find something that would be engaging to their audience and increase repeat daily readers. The solution, created by Richard Adams Locke, and what he wrote became one of the most provocative and notorious stories of all time.[4]

The first installment, which appeared on August 21, 1835, and was titled "Celestial Discoveries," referenced an apparent original publication in the *Edinburgh Journal of Science*. The tale spoke of the discoveries of life on the moon found by astronomer Sir John Herschel. It was true that Herschel had recently made some incredible discoveries from his modest observatory in Cape Town, South Africa, the site of the retelling in *The New York Sun*; however, the rest of the story was pure fiction. It became known as the Moon Hoax.

Over the course of six consecutive days, readers were amazed at the discovery of not just life on the moon, but intelligent life that could be observed through Herschel's (exaggerated) new telescope. Each day the story revealed one more incredible claim after the other, from the observations of colorful plants and bison-like creatures to eventually human forms that resembled beavers living a primitive Native American–like life. It was fascinating.

The story felt like fiction, yet it gave readers something they wanted to believe was true. Many did believe the "news." For most, it confirmed their thoughts about life on the moon, a place they could regularly see but know little else about.

For poet Edgar Allan Poe, it was beyond fiction, and he even hinted that it was inspired by some of his creative writing. He claimed it was fraud and wrote:

> *"Not one person in ten discredited it, and (strangest point of all!) the doubters were chiefly those who doubted without being able to say why—the ignorant, those uninformed in astronomy, people who would not believe because the thing was so novel, so entirely out of the usual way. A grave professor of mathematics in Virginia College told me seriously that he had no doubt of the truth of the whole affair."*

For *The New York Sun*, it was an incredible success. Their daily circulation of 8,000 papers was boosted to more than 19,000 within days. It became the top-selling newspaper in the world, being more popular than *The Times of London*. It is amazing what a little sensationalism can do to promote a news source and *The New York Sun* itself. By portraying stories that blend a bit of truth and fiction, not only did they spur the growth of penny press publications, but they also created the tabloid newspaper.

Tabloid newspapers revealed something else. Readers could be misled simply by the format. Positioning enough truth beside a believable fabrication was deception. Like the misdirection of a magician, readers became so comfortable seeing real news stories one after the other that they did not notice when a proverbial rabbit hopped out of the hat.

Following World War II, television became a mainstay throughout the 1950s. Television stations increased from 6 in 1947 to 96 in 1952. Between 1970 and 1990 the number grew from 875 to 2,277. With more televisions being manufactured, prices for them became lower and they found themselves in the living rooms of urban America. By 1955, half of US households owned a television.

Newspaper readership grew slower than the population, peaking in 1990. After all, how could they compete against television? Even newspapers that published twice daily could not keep pace with television viewers eager for the current news.

Television newscasters like Edward R. Murrow became well-regarded and trusted sources for news following World War II. Murrow created pathways for other TV journalists, including Walter Cronkite.

Walter Cronkite, who hosted the *CBS Evening News* from 1962 to 1981, earned the reputation as the most trusted man in America. The news that he conveyed to Americans each evening as they sat down to learn the activities of the day was authoritative. His career gave way to others, including Tom Brokaw, Dan Rather, Peter Jennings, Katie Couric, Diane Sawyer, and many others.

People relied on the TV news as where they got their information throughout the 1980s and 1990s and into the 2000s. Newspapers were still a reliable source of information among those that had established themselves as trusted, well-researched journalists. They included *The Washington Post*, *The New York Times*, *The Wall Street Journal*, *Los Angeles Times*, and *Chicago Tribune*. All of these had accumulated various awards for their integrity and the thoroughness of the news they presented. Soon, the economics of the newspaper business and, to some extent, also the TV business became a threat to their longevity.

The Internet (Obviously)

The driving force that changed the economics in the early 2000s for both newspapers and television stations was the Internet. The Internet had been around for a little while, but it wasn't until this time that it became common to be in people's homes, thanks in part to companies like America Online (AOL) that offered easy pathways for people to get online and get information. This created more competition for people's attention. The Internet was not just another media channel competing with television and printed newspapers; it was thousands of channels, i.e., websites within the Internet that could draw their attention.

The Internet also changed *how* people gathered information. People were able to seek out the information they were looking for rather than have it pushed to them through TV or the printed pages of the newspaper. They could be more deliberate in what they were looking for and find it in a wider variety of places. As a result, newspapers and television stations lost influence over controlling the narrative of the day or over being the primary source of facts that they were presenting to the American public. Now the American public was empowered. Generally, we thought this was a good thing. People could find what they wanted when they needed it. They could verify facts, and often these facts were from bona fide sources, like books, universities, government agencies, newspapers, and television stations that were the trusted curators of facts and news at the time. However, times change.

The Internet was born from an idea at the US Department of Defense within its Defense Advanced Research Projects Agency, known as DARPA, in the 1970s. Its purpose was to create a decentralized communications network that connected many different computer systems together. The network first connected university computers to military bases, and by 1982 the Internet Protocol Suite was standardized, facilitating the connection of other commercial computer systems.

While the Internet helped connect computers for the purposes of communication, it was not until the development of the World Wide Web (the familiar "`http://www.`") by Tim Berners-Lee in December 1990 that things began to happen. The World Wide Web that he developed allowed the creation of websites and, with the Hypertext

Transfer Protocol, information could be shared and hyperlinked between computers. He hosted the first website server where he worked at CERN (also known as the European Organization for Nuclear Research) in Geneva, Switzerland. The server was a lone NeXT computer, which is still on display at CERN.

The Internet, with its function of both communication through email and hosting information, was soon on its way toward transforming the distribution of information, much like the invention of the printing press. Beginning in the late 1980s and early 1990s, access to the Internet became commercially available—no longer the privilege of those in government or academic institutions. In 1998, 23% of US households had access; by 2003, that figure had reached 50%. Currently, 98% of US adults report having access to the Internet in their homes or on their mobile phones.[5]

With more people online gaining rapid access to the news, the decline in print newspapers was inevitable. In 1990, there were 1,611 daily newspapers in the United States; by 2009, the number was 1,387. Currently, there are 938 newspapers.

Many of those newspapers also distribute their news online; for example, *The New York Times* has 250,000 print subscribers and 11.3 million online subscribers. However, the percentage of the population getting their news from legacy newspapers is significantly smaller than it was 25 years ago.

The circulation of newspapers tells a similar story. According to a Pew Research Center study, newspapers peaked between 1960 and 1990, having a total circulation of daily newspapers of about 60 million. It declined rapidly from then to 45 million in 2010, 24 million in 2020, and today is estimated to be below 15 million. To put this into perspective, the current US adult population is 265 million. Assuming most of those people have a desire to get news from somewhere, we know from these numbers that it is not from newspapers and, as we showed earlier, is also not from traditional television news broadcasts. So where?

Trusted Institutions

Governments were so trusted at one point that many cultures in history looked to their leaders for answers to natural disasters, famine, and war. Many cultures picked their leaders with the belief that those individuals were divinely chosen as representatives of their gods. Held high in society, they held secret knowledge. Some societies sacrificed animals, infant children, and warriors in hopes of improving their lives and staving off intruders, storms, and locusts. They were trusted.

But what happens to society when the truth becomes negotiable? In the United States, in a span of a little over a single generation, our trust in government has plummeted. We have gone from believing what we read in newspapers or hear from our own governments to now doubting what we see with our own eyes. Data from a Gallup study shows that trust in the federal government to handle domestic problems was at a 70% rate in 1972. It dropped to 58% in 2000 and 46% in 2010. Currently, it is around 37%. A similar study from the Pew Research Center showed trust in the federal government plummeted from 75% in 1958 to just 22% as of May 2024.

The decline was driven by a few factors, including the Vietnam War in the 1960s and the Watergate scandal in the 1970s. Both events created distrust. The Vietnam War was tragic, and many Americans questioned the role the United States was playing in the conflict. The medium of television gave people a more personal view. The candor of embedded journalists displaced the authority of the government, which was losing control of the narrative. As a result, people felt a disconnect between what their government was telling them and what they were watching on television. Their distrust was verifiable.

The Watergate scandal a few years later continued to erode trust in the government. The story was about a break-in at the Democratic National Committee headquarters in the Watergate office complex in

Washington, DC, in June 1972. The people involved were attempting to steal documents and place wiretaps on the phones in the building on behalf of President Nixon. What happened following that was a cover-up from Nixon and the White House, where they destroyed evidence, tried to influence the investigation, and obscured the investigative actions by the United States Department of Justice. This came to light due to the incredible investigative journalism by *The Washington Post* journalists Bob Woodward and Carl Bernstein. Senate hearings followed and eventually, the president resigned from office. It led to other members of the government serving time in prison for the cover-up, notably US Attorney General John Mitchell.

For some, Watergate confirmed politicians could be dishonest. For others, it revealed that not only could individual politicians lie, but the *entire government* could lie. One benefit of the scandal was that it boosted the trust the public had in investigative journalism. Without it, the true story might have been hidden. For the moment, trust in investigative journalism and the quality newspapers that provided it was much higher than trust in government.

Influencers, Your New Neighbors

Melanskia, an Amish grandmother, is strolling through the aisles of Costco. She is sharing in her Instagram video the ingredients we might all find in everyday products. Synthetic ingredients that are "like glue to your internal filter." Melanskia has several similar videos and more than 350,000 followers. She shares her back-to-basics food philosophy. She is pleasantly charming. And if you happen to not live on an Amish farm like her, well, she has a great supplement for you that will do the same thing for your healthy diet. The supplement. That should have been the first tell.

If we journey back through time, influencers might have appeared very different than they do today, yet they served the same role. Older generations might recall when there were only three broadcast networks, a daily newspaper or two (depending on the size of the town where they lived), and a couple of radio stations. These "traditional" outlets provided most of the information they needed about day-to-day activities in their community. What they could not find in those sources, they could learn in person by meeting friends at the local diner, bowling alley, or hair salon. In those days, you could learn a lot about what happened at last night's city council meeting just by chatting with people at the grocery store. News, beyond what was pushed to you from those traditional sources, came by talking to your neighbors. Information was personal.

The Internet closed our differences in geography. It made it possible to know what was happening on the other side of the planet in a way that was different than reading about it in the newspapers or watching it on television. In its early days, Twitter was used to share local news. Want to know the current score of your high school football game? Well, Twitter could help you with that. Twitter was a citizen news source, providing real-time tweets of events like the 2009 Miracle on the Hudson plane landing. It also provided a platform for activists, playing a role in the Arab Spring[6] and separately the Me Too and Black Lives Matter movements.

This use of social media is not all driven by online personalities, but it does give some people a place to grow an outsized following that previously was reserved for known celebrities. The larger platforms are among those that have been around the longest, such as Facebook, X (Twitter), Instagram, TikTok, and YouTube. Most of these larger platforms have *billions* of active users with billions of monthly interactions. Facebook alone has over 3 billion active users and 10.5 billion monthly interactions. To extend their reach, many influencers also maintain a presence on other smaller platforms, like Mastodon, Bluesky, and Snapchat.

The line between today's influencers, their sponsors, and controversial topics has deep roots. Influencers existed long before the Internet and social media, originally in the form of celebrity product endorsements on television. In the late 1950s, Rod Serling was the host and creator of *The Twilight Zone*, a science fiction television show. Each episode was a self-contained story with a different cast and plot. Often at the end of each episode, Serling appeared on screen to narrate the story's conclusion. He also did something unique at the time: he suggested viewers buy Chesterfield King cigarettes. Chesterfield King was the show's sponsor, meaning it paid to be mentioned on the program, and Serling was its influencer.

Television became a primary marketing tool for companies at the time when 75% of US households owned a TV. Broadcasters were vying for attention, and marketing departments wanted to associate their brands with popular programming. However, some viewers, in particular parents, voiced complaints about some of the programming they felt was inappropriate. The industry, fearing direct government censorship, created the Television Code of 1952.

In addition to creating programming suitable for children, the act also limited the portrayal of other negative content. It created moral content standards ranging from profanity, sex, religion, and other indecent behaviors that were otherwise deemed offensive to the mid-century conservative American public (fortunately for Rod Serling, smoking was not yet considered a moral vice).

Corporations took notice and began self-censoring by way of their sponsorships. None wanted to be associated with seemingly controversial topics. For a show like *The Twilight Zone* and Rod Serling, this was a challenge. Serling, who also served as the writer for many of the episodes, used the show as a platform for debate on many controversial topics, testing the limits of the Television Code. In a clever way, he used *The Twilight Zone* to tackle some bold ideas, things like McCarthyism, racism, conformity, and the fear of nuclear war. He used science fiction and fantasy to comment on the social and political climate, making it more of a thought-provoking show without directly portraying these topics as news. He was an influencer ahead of his time.

While Serling had to navigate the Television Code among a growing and curious 1950s audience, influencers today are not bound by those same rules. The Television Code is overseen by the Federal Communications Commission (FCC), and it still has the power to censor inappropriate and misleading television. However, the FCC does not regulate the Internet or the content that anyone, including influencers, broadcasts. This makes it easier for influencers to go beyond the facts and go beyond the news.

There are a few problems with influencers as a trusted source of information. First, influencers rely on boosting their online rankings as measured by the number of followers. In addition, the content they post also gets measured with the count of "likes" and "shares" in near real time. Imagine if you could see the same for an online news article from *The New York Times*, or while watching the *CBS Evening News*. For viewers of social media content, these numbers matter. They suggest trust and validity in a way that is not always correlated with facts and truth, especially among a growing subset of influencers known as *news influencers*.

Going viral for reporting the news seemed like an impossibility for traditional newspaper and television journalists. It would require a story so compelling that people would share it as a historic event. And it couldn't be something that was created to be provocative or to generate a response among readers and viewers. Remember, traditional media is subject to regulations from the FCC and also the policies of their own organizations that provided guidance on fact-checking and misleading the public. News influencers have fewer of these barriers.

News influencers are a relatively new subset of online personalities, and they represent your new virtual neighbors for sources of information. The Pew Research Center only began recognizing them in its research in 2024, following years of research about social media suggesting that more people were getting their news from social media platforms. Its most recent research shows that 21% of people regularly get their news from these sites. The number is higher among those 18 to 29 years old (38%).

The gravitation toward social media platforms as a place where people would get their news is a natural evolution. People are already online, and it adds another level of convenience by not needing to switch from one application to another. The blending of social topics (entertainers, celebrities, fashion) with "hard" news topics (economy, politics, health, science) can impact how people perceive information, especially when the two combine, like when celebrities are providing healthcare advice. Another shift is a result of the post-pandemic effect.

The COVID-19 pandemic created a lot of discussion about which healthcare sources could be trusted. From the traditional news sources to television and social media, there was a lot of debate about what was factual and what was not, including information coming from the government itself. The US government often communicated information that conflicted with other government agencies.

As the Pew Research Center study goes deeper, it shows that there are other factors too that cause this break with traditional news sources. Fifty-two percent of survey respondents indicated that they *preferred* news influencers because they were independent and *not* part of any other news organization or the government. The anchor of truth had moved. They also thought that the news influencers were more authentic, and perhaps this leads to a higher level of trust. Quite simply, they are seeking a fresh voice and a perception of unbiasedness. Someone who will talk directly to them has garnered a new voice of trust.

However, there is another problem for influencers and online content creators. Given that they are not part of a larger news organization that might consider reputational risks, or those subject to the FCC, they have more liberty with the facts. A 2024 UNESCO survey of 500 online content creators from 45 countries found that only 36.9% fact-checked their information before posting, citing that if they trusted their sources before, then there was little need to check the details. How did they trust the source? Likes and views. Of the respondents, 41.6% referred to likes and views as the *primary* factor in determining their source's credibility.

The Noise of the Infodemic

Information from traditional sources is collapsing. Like watching an old dam giving way under the pressure of a storm-driven flooding river, you can see how its failure to hold back the water creates a rush of more water into a river. Through our history, we have built foundations and structures to shape how we capture, store, use, and share information. Like the water building up in the river, those structures can no longer function as they once did because how we use information has changed. How we gather information is changing. How information is created, more at the digital hands of AI, is changing. The river is rising, and we need to rise with it.

Information and the hyper-news cycle, the rapid increase in which a news story rises to our attention, becomes part of our public discourse, and then fades to obscurity, are taxing our ability to process information. Here today and in a week, a day, or an hour, it will all be over.

Previously, we looked to our trusted information sources to help us navigate. The evening news anchor, our local government, and a trusted voice among many gave us guidance. The world, of course, is changing, and those voices we trust are harder to find. Melanskia, the

Amish grandmother who gives us healthy advice, at first seems helpful. However, the Amish influencer is not Amish. She is not even real. Instead, she is AI-generated, taking advantage of our trust. We trust farmers and the Amish to give us advice about food and natural diets. We trust our elders. They have wisdom, and we need that type of wisdom in our lives from time to time. Her digital identity lives on a platform that in early 2024 wrote about its commitment to identifying and labeling AI content, yet years later Melanskia has no such label. Meta in particular encourages AI content using Meta AI Image Generators to promote its platforms, to create content, and to serve millions of viewers. When what we really are experiencing is just more information, more discourse, and more distraction from the truth we need.

Key Takeaways

- The trust collapse is real and unprecedented. Although at times in history information was segregated, new forms of communication—from the written word to the printing press and the Internet—usually expanded trusted knowledge to a wider group of people.
- Trust in governments is in decline. The number of people in the United States who trust the government has plummeted from 75% in 1958 to just 22% in 2024, a breakdown that parallels the rise of social media and the decline of traditional media.
- Traditional media, previously gatekeepers to researched news, are collapsing. Newspaper circulation dropped from 60 million in 1990 to 15 million today.
- Social media influencers are enabled with new AI tools and access to large audiences, creating a new source of information.

Notes

1. There are more than 1,000 handwritten manuscripts and fragments of Homer's work, and there continues to be debate about which versions, or pieces, are most authentic to the original story.
   "The Transmission and Reception of Homer's Works," *The University of Chicago Library*, `https://www.lib.uchicago.edu/collex/exhibits/homer-print-transmission-and-reception-homers-works/homer-print`
2. Elizabeth Webster, "How Ben Franklin Invented the Library as We Know It," *Smithsonian Magazine*, April/May 2024, `https://www.smithsonianmag.com/history/how-ben-franklin-invented-library-as-we-know-it-180983983`
3. Ronald P. Formisano, *For the People: American Populist Movements from the Revolution to the 1850s* (Chapel Hill: University of North Carolina Press, 2008), 111–12.
4. Locke was also a descendant of philosopher John Locke, which may have added to his initial credibility.
   István Kornél Vida, "The 'Great Moon Hoax' of 1835," *Hungarian Journal of English and American Studies* 18, no. 1/2 (2012): 431–41, `http://www.jstor.org/stable/43488485`
5. Rafi Goldberg, "New NTIA Data Show 13 Million More Internet Users in the U.S. in 2023 than 2021," *National Telecommunications and Information Administration*, June 6, 2024, `https://www.ntia.gov/blog/2024/new-ntia-data-show-13-million-more-internet-users-us-2023-2021`
6. While most of the participants in the Arab Spring protests that took place between December 2010 and December 2012 relied on television and word of mouth, what is important is that the use of social media such as Twitter and Facebook helped reach people during a time when governments were attempting to suppress news coverage. A study of tweets and links showed that 13 percent of participants relied on social media.
   Alex Remington, "New Media and Conflict after the Arab Spring," *The Journalist's Resource*, August 6, 2012, `https://journalistsresource.org/economics/new-media-sms-conflict-after-the-arab-spring`

Chapter 2

The Negotiated Truth

". . .officials should have thought twice before mingling this news technique with fiction so terrifying. Horror for the sake of the thrill has been legitimately exploited. . ."

—The New York Times

It is Halloween Eve in 1938. If that date is familiar to you, it is because you know the story of the most well-known radio hoax of all time: *The War of the Worlds*. Orson Welles, then only 23, led listeners of the *Mercury Theatre on the Air* show through an adapted tale from the 1898 H. G. Wells novel of the same name. It was the story of a frightening invasion. There were aliens from Mars landing in suburban New Jersey and eventually spreading across the country. People listened—and panicked.

There were thousands of phone calls to the police station. People fled from their homes in fear, many wrapping towels across their faces to protect them from the *alien gas*. The aliens at this point had allegedly killed the reporter; no one really knew, as the radio feed from the field reporter suddenly just . . .stopped. Another reporter for the broadcast told how the military was fighting back but was overpowered by superior Martian weapons. The horror listeners felt caused hundreds to call *The New York Times* and *The Daily News*—the prominent newspapers at the time—to ask what to do, where to go, and how to survive.

By some accounts, millions were listening. Five college students in North Carolina fainted, while others struggled to call home to be rescued. A woman in Boston, declared she could see the fire from over the horizon. As the hour-long broadcast closed, Orson calmed the listeners. He said, "We annihilated the world before your very ears and utterly destroyed the CBS. You will be relieved, I hope, to learn that we didn't mean it, and that both institutions are still open for business." In other words, it was just a radio drama, and the invasion was a hoax. But the real hoax was something else completely different.

The following day there was outrage when people read about it in the newspapers. Yes, the newspapers. *The New York Times'* article simply titled "Terror by Radio" scolded the radio broadcast, stating "that thousands, from one end of the country to the other, were frightened out of their senses . . . taxing the police and hospitals, confusing traffic and choking the usual means of communication." Further, "What began as 'entertainment' might readily have ended in disaster." It was irresponsible. It was recklessly mimicking the news. The real news.

The Daily News' leading story was titled "Fake 'War' On Radio Spreads Panic Over U.S." It depicted the stories of the chaos—churches being filled by those seeking protection, at least 15 people asking for treatment for shock at Newark's St. Michael's Hospital, and hundreds of physicians and nurses calling the New York City Department of Health volunteering to rush in to aid the victims of the Martian attack. The side stories told similar first-person accounts involving the fire departments, city hall, and the National Guard. The message was the same. How could they, the people in charge of radio, put so many people in harm's way? Reassuring the newspaper readers was an accompanying story about Senator Clyde Herring, a Democrat from Iowa, who planned to introduce a bill in Congress "controlling such abuses as was heard over the radio." *The New York*

Times reported the Federal Communications Commission (FCC) would review the transcripts and determine what actions it might take.

The story of the greatest radio hoax of all time—that most of us heard in journalism or communication classes, and that is often cited as the best example of what not to do—is not what it seems. The story of the hoax is a hoax itself, driven by misinformation.

What the Newspapers Left Out

In 1938 there was no AI, but misinformation and the fight for the negotiated truth were as real as they are today. The newspapers were battling for people's attention with radio stations, and the opportunity to discredit them as a reliable news source seemed too good to pass up. Radio had grown in popularity throughout the 1930s, with 90% of US households owning a radio by 1940 compared to 40% in 1930. Radio, of course, could offer a more immediate connection to its news audience but lacked the newsrooms of the papers. The competition was dubbed the press-radio war. At the time newspapers banned the Associated Press (AP), which gathered and distributed news to newspapers, from sharing news with radio stations.

When the radio broadcast of *The War of the Worlds* occurred, it seemed easy to attack them. However, the anecdotal stories of the panic were either one-off descriptions of the people who missed the few brief announcements throughout the program that it was just a drama, or something worse. Perhaps the newspapers fabricated listeners' reactions. There is no way to confirm that. However, there is some other useful data.

The radio rating company C.E. Hooper surveyed 5,000 households on the evening of October 20, 1938, and found that 98% of radio listeners were *not* listening to CBS Radio's *The War of the Worlds*. They were listening to the much more popular *The Chase and Sanborn Hour* on NBC Radio. During this time, known as the golden age of radio, an estimated 28 million households could have tuned in to the broadcast. According to the data from C.E. Hooper, the CBS share of the listeners that evening was a mere 2%, or roughly 500,000 across the *entire* United States. Could some believe it was real? Yes. Could thousands in the local New York and New Jersey area panic to the extreme that the newspapers reported? No.

The newspapers in their critique of radio were using a technique that remains familiar—the pairing of fear and partial truths. At the time there was a heightened level of fear from the very real news readers were exposed to from the brewing war in Europe. Nazi Germany had just invaded Austria and parts of Czechoslovakia in 1938 and was provoking its other neighbors. A year earlier in 1937, the Hindenburg disaster occurred in New Jersey, which was historically reported by a radio reporter on the scene—a tactic that Orson Welles replicated for *The War of the Worlds*. It was familiar, memorable, and believable. For the newspapers, they saw this as exploitative, but it was also a tactic they too were using to stir the emotional response of their readers. Like the 2023 photo of the Pentagon explosion, there were relatable facts—the 9/11 terrorist attacks, the war in Ukraine—that drew our attention. In 1938 some felt that same fight-or-flight response either from misunderstanding the radio broadcast or simply reading the newspaper story about it the following day.

Later they likely felt another emotional response: anger. Newspapers of the past and future were not immune to this method of gaining readers. As social media continues to change news cycles and our attention to content shortens, the remaining newspapers have adapted more to its style than to their traditional roots. Attention and time now matter more.

The story of *The War of the Worlds* reveals something crucial: the misinformation was not the fake Martian invasion; it was the fake panic.

The Whole Story

Newspapers in their reporting of the story fell into the cherry-picking bias—they selectively chose the anecdotal stories of people's reactions and panic over a wider and more objective story. Were the "panic" newspaper headlines just too tempting, too engaging to overlook? Newspapers were, after all, in the business of selling newspapers.

The ratings agency data from C.E. Hooper could have been a counter fact; recall that their survey found only 2% of people were listening to CBS that evening, and none reported they were listening to the news. They reported listening to a "play" or "The Orson Welles Show."[1] It is possible journalists, as a group, were subject to their own confirmation bias—the behavior in which the only information used is, knowingly or unknowingly, the information that confirms one's preconceived beliefs.

The news of the panic was not just reported in *The New York Times* or *The Daily News*. The story travelled to hundreds of newspapers, like *The Washington Times*, *The Philadelphia Inquirer*, and the *Atlanta Daily World*. It was sensational news that editors of all those newspapers readily accepted: the panic, the critique of radio that was taking away their advertising revenues and readers.

The only balanced reporting of *The War of the Worlds* came two weeks later from another publication called *Broadcasting*. And if you were to believe it was a journal for radio station owners and their advertisers, then you would be exactly right. *Broadcasting* was a twice-monthly trade journal that wrote about the new prospering industry of radio. Readers could learn which new stations were launching, how the government was responding to its oversight, and ratings of stations and programming. The latter determined how much companies were charged for advertising. Radio also had a vested interest in protecting its airwaves, and a disparaging reputation for causing public panic might cause advertisers to flee.

The story noted the facts, and it also noted the *responsible* parts of the story that were untold in the newspapers, such as the fact that during the broadcast there were four announcements that it was a fictional drama. There was also downplaying of the extent that it caused a panic, adding that they ". . .were amazed that sane citizens could be so influenced by the dramatization of a 50-year-old fable." They wrote that the review by the FCC of listener letters was 50-50, praising and criticizing the broadcast (did people really write to the FCC to praise a radio show?) Further, CBS Radio apologized, regretting that some listeners "mistook fantasy for fact," and after all, *The Mercury Theatre on the Air* show was poorly rated and had few listeners. How much harm could they have caused, they professed? So few listeners, just 2% as verified by C.E. Hooper—a survey and rating organization exclusively for radio.

What we know is *The War of the Worlds* created a truth not just about radio, but also a foretelling of all new media that would follow. It will be distrusted. It will disrupt the legacy institutions. It will create criticism. Is the new medium better than the old? What is given up in the transition from one to the other, and is coexistence possible? In the case of radio and newspapers, coexistence reshaped how each adapted—newspapers rarely focus on entertainment as they did when they published serialized fiction. Radio focuses more on entertainment and less on deep journalistic reporting.

In 1938 these lines were less clear. The radio was in fact a rich source of news, as were newspapers. In the weeks and months that followed, the truth of October 30 and the broadcast's impact were negotiated in public. Years later, while by most reports the panic was not a panic at all, the real answer requires perspective—it caused panic for some, at least hundreds and maybe thousands of people. But, as a percentage of the 28 million possible listeners, that perspective is a small number.

When the truth needs to be negotiated, we need to first ask what is the real truth?

When Truth Needs a Referee

Then it was simpler. There were only a few sources of verification: the call logs to police stations and newspapers, along with the surveys from listeners. The intervention of the government and the Federal Trade Commission added data points and credibility to the conclusions. Eventually people trusted the newspapers to tell them the truth over the perceived lies of radio. The newspapers controlled the narrative and had decades of credibility, and their publications far outnumbered radio stations.

In the AI era we face the same type of problem of who and what to believe as those in 1938. Different audiences on radio and newspapers might have had different perceived realities of the events, but just from those two sources. Today, given our individualized AI-curated news feeds from several online apps, most people might be presented with different realities of a particular event. You might even be given the opposite "perspective" from your neighbors. These are further amplified by algorithms programmed not to provide you with the truth, but to keep you online and engaged as long as possible. Tracking your past behaviors, customized news that keeps you digging for the truth or sharing with others is what they are designed to do and how they continue to collect your data. In this era, we do not seek the news objectively. The news finds you.

When we find news, or when it is presented as an integrated part of our online experience, we need to be our own truth referees.

Establishment news sources like newspapers, television news, and governments have been waning both in numbers and in levels of trust. Trust in government in particular has fallen, as we noted, to an astonishingly low level, with only 22% of survey respondents indicating trust. And while trust in the government decreases, the government has had influence in the past in attempting to regulate misinformation online following the same reasoning the FCC uses against TV and radio. Broadcasters under FCC rules must avoid causing substantial public harm and are prohibited from giving false content during news programming. Platforms like Facebook and Twitter in their early days had similar expectations and, prior to 2025, had various attempts at self-regulation. Since then, we have been our best truth referees, but it has its challenges.

For generations we have (mostly) relied on pillars of truth, and in the AI era we need to adapt to new methods of source verification. Radio listeners could dial surf to another channel to check information, just as a reader could look at a few different newspapers. Choices gave opportunities for verification.

Among the many considerations is this: who benefits from the increased volume of AI-infused misinformation? Are they nation-states streaming out propaganda? Are they influencers trying to grow new revenue sources from advertisers? Are corporations trying to capture the loyalty of their customers?

Like in the 1930s and 1940s, newspaper criticism of radio and eventually television was about money. Each was losing customers to the other and revenues along with them. "Follow the money," that sage phrase, has relevance in the AI era. Are the changes we are seeing with AI about Google, Meta, xAI, Microsoft, and Amazon controlling the online marketplace? Presenting the "favorable" news as they chase our advertising revenue dollars? And does this impact the objectivity of the news we see? The answer is likely yes and a topic we will explore further later in this book.

What Is Truth?

> *"To say of what is that it is not, or of what is not that it is, is false, while to say of what is that it is, and of what is not that it is not, is true."*
>
> —Aristotle (*Metaphysics*)

How do we define the truth, and does everyone operate the same way when it comes to what they know and believe? Further, what are the underpinnings of our belief systems and how are those changing because of AI? You may know from experiences like these that people's adherence to belief systems varies, but we all have some commonality in how we arrive at our version of the truth. To understand how people accept the truth, we need to examine the most common frameworks of truth and verification.

Correspondence Theory

This is the most common theory of truth. With its roots in Plato and Aristotle, this type of truth verification relies on evidence in the observable, tangible world. The evidence is not limited to physical objects, but more broadly to things that can be proven with data. It is the basis of the Scientific Method and is widely used in empirical research. A theory or statement is true if it corresponds to an objective external reality, i.e., there is empirical evidence.

Inherent in correspondence theory is the need for and acceptance of the credibility of the reference source. When the source has a high level of authority—again, these are the traditional sources we have been discussing in these pages, like governments, academic institutions, legacy newspapers, and television—then this increases its acceptance as true.

Coherence Theory

This is a theory that is more common in law and mathematics and relies on logic. A statement is true when it is logically consistent and coheres within a broader system or network of beliefs. It follows a path of reasoning, and the validity of arguments depends on the internal consistency of how well they fit within an established set of rules or beliefs.

Pragmatic Theory

This is more related to real-life experiences. It holds true when it provides outcomes that effectively work. Does it meet expectations?

Consensus Theory

This is the claim that something is true when most people, that is, the consensus, also believe it to be true. This is demonstrated in science when there are ambiguous results about a particular set of experiments, but the *consensus* of the scientists agrees on one truth. Consensus theory is very important for social media. Similar to the game show contestant, people use "likes" and "shares" as a proxy for group consensus. While this increases confidence in the truth of the information for the viewer, it is, of course, not guaranteed to be true.

Consciously or unconsciously, we all use a variation of the aforementioned theories to determine what we feel is true. Whether we are deep thinkers like Plato or Aristotle, or we just arrive at a gut feeling about something in our mind, these mechanisms are working behind the scenes to give us clues. However, we do not have the luxury of time in our online experiences to be deliberate philosophers. In the AI era, information moves faster than a clay tablet or printed newspaper. Our minds are overloaded, overworked, and purposely being wrangled by media to command our attention. Our critical-thinking skills are derailed. As a result, sometimes we give up trying to verify information and accept what we see or read as true. After all, this is how most of us learned throughout our entire lives. For generations this is how we have been conditioned to trust.

Is the Moon Real? Is the Earth Flat?

Accept that the moon is in fact real, and the Earth is not flat. But if you are searching for the truth in the noise, then these concepts might be up for discussion, at least among particular people. Most people know these are truths, but why? What is the basis for these truths?

Imagine you have a friend who, out of academic curiosity, asks how we know that the moon really exists. We take it for granted from the things we've been taught in school, but how could we answer this question on our own? The first thing we would ask is, what do you think the moon is if it is not a real object out in space rotating around the Earth? Is it a projection or a flat object suspended in space?

First, we could use the correspondence theory, perform an experiment, and see how well the evidence corresponds to the idea that the moon is real. Our observation of the moon is a strong piece of evidence. We know it appears regularly, and if we had a telescope, we could look at the edges of the moon to see the shadows as the sunlight beams across the craters. When we look again an hour later, the shadows have changed, both demonstrating the moon is not a flat disc and that it is rotating. The moon is real.

We could also employ consensus theory. Most people accept that the moon does exist. And by conducting a consensus survey among our friends, we would have agreement that the moon, in fact, is real and rotates around the Earth. So, there are two very easy ways to verify that the moon is real. But what about more complicated topics?

The Flat Earth Society claims its roots date back to the early 1800s when it was founded by Samuel Birley Rowbotham. He was an

English inventor and first wrote of the flat earth in a pamphlet in 1849 based on his literal interpretations of Bible passages. The Biblical interpretation was a result of the poetic language used as it was translated over time. For example, in the book of Ezekiel there is a reference to ". . .four corners of the land."[2]

While the idea has long existed, most people accept that the Earth is not flat, although there was a resurgence of this belief around 2017 when Netflix released a documentary titled *Behind the Curve*. The University of New Hampshire published the results of its 2021 science knowledge survey, called POLES, and reported that 10% of people believed the Earth was flat. Another poll using a slightly different methodology conducted by YouGov in the United Kingdom in 2019 showed the number closer to 3%.

Again, consider that same academically curious friend asking, "How do we know the Earth is not flat?" The evidence-based approach is to look at a sailing ship on the horizon as it is sailing away. Instead of it getting smaller and smaller in the distance, as you would expect on a flat surface, you could observe the boat gradually disappearing while the mast remains visible. If following boats to the horizon is too difficult, try sitting on a beach watching the sunset and, at the moment it disappears, climb up a (rather convenient) stepladder and you will see the sun again. This can only happen when the Earth is curved. Other evidence could include observing a lunar eclipse showing the curvature of the Earth's shadow as it is cast upon the moon (which we have now established exists).

Another approach is to use the coherence theory—does the truth of a round Earth align with other beliefs without creating contradictions? The latter is important because we can sometimes get part of a belief to fit another fact, but it must not cause other facts to fall out of alignment. If a person could reliably track the flight path of a passenger plane from Tokyo to New York and its path over the Arctic, it would look like a detour on a flat Earth. If that same person could observe the fuel logs from the plane, they could see that the apparent "curved" path used less fuel than another that took a seemingly straight line. The curvature of the Earth fits this information. Only a sphere could account for a shorter path.

Of course, there is also the consensus approach. Most people believe the Earth is not flat. If you could travel, you would know this is accepted in different cultures and parts of the world. However, this is the difficulty of verifying "large" facts like the shape of the Earth. For most, the observable evidence and even the consensus evidence are far from attainable—a flight around the world would suffice. When it comes to misinformation online, simple untruths are easily shattered. The ones that persist are more complicated to prove—the ones that fall conveniently between the slightly believable and the nearly impossible to verify. The bigger the misinformation feat, sometimes the longer and more difficult it can be to overcome.

The journey of the Flat Earth Society and its believers from obscurity in the 1800s to mainstream acknowledgment in a movie is important. Until the mid-2000s, their beliefs would remain only among a small group. Picture a weekly meeting at the local British pub. A few members would share their latest thoughts, maybe attracting a few new members who heard about it through conversation. The group would be limited in its reach to new members and its ability to spread its ideas. Only organizations with enough funding could write more than a pamphlet or advertise in newspapers. Small ideas remained small.

The Internet, and in particular social media, changed how people could connect to others across town or across the globe based on obscure ideology. In the early days of Facebook, it was hard to find people with similar beliefs, and it usually required a friend-of-a-friend introduction. Building groups using this process took time and commitment.

Conveniently, in 2009, Facebook added a very important feature: the "Like" and "Share" buttons. Not only did these let your friends know your interests, but they also let Facebook know them. Its algorithm—that mathematical set of rules measuring the probability that you would read about a person or topic—was getting *smarter* with every click. For Flat Earthers, whose numbers were small, social media suddenly provided a way to find people like them. Social media platforms were suggesting them, in effect providing that introduction once required a pub visit or a personal introduction. Opaque ideas and contested truths felt bigger than they were because, for the people that experienced the transformation of social media, they were now experiencing a new social media phenomenon called echo chambers.

To the Moon

Doubt of the Moon Landing in 1969 is among the longest-surviving pieces of misinformation. Millions of people watched on television, a highly trusted news source, which captivated the attention of 530 million viewers. All the other news mediums—newspapers, radio stations, academia—told and retold the same story of the great American achievement of putting people on the moon. How could people not believe it was true?

In 1961, President Kennedy, while addressing the United States Congress, announced the goal of landing on the moon. He termed it a ". . .battle between freedom and tyranny," a response to the Soviet Union's achievement in launching Sputnik in 1957, the first Earth satellite. For most of the 1960s Americans learned about the Apollo space program that employed 400,000 people and resulted in the Apollo 11 moon landing in 1969. Americans celebrated the achievement and missions that followed until its conclusion in 1972. In total, 12 astronauts reached the moon, performed scientific experiments, gathered rock samples, and returned home. But back home, things were changing. Trust was changing.

The Watergate scandal mentioned earlier contributed to eroding trust beginning in 1972. Over the next few years, people would learn about the connection of the burglars to the President, some of whom were former CIA agents. The speculation, the conspiracies, and the eventual revelation of a cover-up by the White House changed the trust people gave to their government. People felt they could not trust what they heard from their elected leaders and their administration. During the years of World War II and the time that followed, people had higher trust in the government to provide safety and guidance. Following the Watergate scandal, the erosion of trust was extending into other topics like the moon landing. What if it were not true?

We can employ the frameworks mentioned earlier in a similar fashion, and we would arrive at the same place. The moon landings were true based on the logical possibility (the Soviet Union and the United States launched rockets into space), evidence (photos, testimony, witnesses of launches), and consensus. And yes, the consensus was high regarding the belief, but the doubters were indirectly encouraged by a government that now seemed less reliable and defensive of the truth.

More than 50 years later, 5–10% of people in the United States believe the moon landing was faked, depending on the methodology of the survey. What is most interesting is the difference between age groups. Older Americans are less likely to believe in the hoax, presumably because they witnessed the news as it was happening in their youth. However, 18% of younger people, those aged 18–34, doubt the moon landing. Why? Social media brings people together in ways that were never imagined. Those following the moon landing hoax also found their echo chamber.

A Simpler Explanation

In 1969 it was very difficult to fabricate fiction as truth. Computer-generated imagery (CGI) would not reach its filmmaking stride until the 1990s, with movies like *Jurassic Park* and *Toy Story*. The best that could be created at the time was the 1968 movie, *2001: A Space Odyssey*. Not surprisingly, some believed that Stanley Kubrick, the creator of that movie, was also hired to fake the moon landing footage. It is convenient to connect Kubrick's movie to the photos from the moon, and this is what we tend to do when we encounter new information that does not align with other known facts.

The "truth" of the moon landing, if it were real, might be hard for people to accept, and a simpler explanation—that it is just another version of a movie like *2001: A Space Odyssey*—is easier to accept. Connecting two ideas like this is a mental shortcut known as the *illusory correlation bias*. Social media can amplify the connections, validating one's beliefs. Recall that social media algorithms are structured to keep people engaged, and this is best done by showing familiar topics that viewers "like" and willingly "share" with others. Although there are thousands of photos and interviews from the Apollo missions, which are often recycled both in defense of and to debunk the moon landing hoax, AI offers a new opportunity to look more deeply into the evidence. That is, AI-generated evidence can appear compelling and convincing.

Usually, conspiracy theories rely on inconsistencies in existing evidence and then question those gaps. AI designed to be divisive is a useful tool for just this purpose.

Prompt: Provide a concise list of the moon landing evidence and the gaps conspiracy theorists exploit.

Gaps Conspiracy Theorists Exploit:

- *Waving flag: Appears to move due to inertia and rigid pole design, not wind (there's no atmosphere).*

- *No stars in photos: Camera exposure was set for the bright lunar surface; faint stars were not captured.*
- *Odd shadows / lighting: Misinterpreted perspective and uneven terrain create the illusion of multiple light sources.*
- *Van Allen radiation belts: Mischaracterized as lethal barriers; Apollo transited them quickly with minimal exposure.*
- *Film technology skepticism: Doubt that 1960s technology could achieve the feat despite documented aerospace capabilities.*
- *Missing original tapes: Some backup telemetry tapes were erased, fueling distrust despite multiple preserved copies elsewhere.*
- *Perceived political motive: Suspicion that Cold War pressures incentivized a staged event.*
- *Scale of coordination disbelief: Assumption that such a secret couldn't be kept, ironically ignoring the massive global visibility.*

The core pattern: conspiracy theories thrive where there's a gap between what experts know and what the public can directly verify, especially when the topic is emotionally or politically charged.

AI can also generate completely new ideas to convince people of an alternative truth. It might suggest a deathbed whistleblower testimony or found footage confirming the fake landing. AI can, of course, also create this type of realistic evidence. It can even provide a helpful marketing strategy to guide bad actors on how best to post it online, targeting specific groups.

For everything there is an explanation. We tend to want those explanations to be simple and align with our previous pillars of truth, linking one to the other, rather than taking one giant step. This is how we often accept new truths. It is also how we can avoid accepting things that are difficult to validate. AI can help reaffirm those truths, and it can also show us plausible ways to simply discourage us from the truth.

Alternative Facts

> *"Who controls the past controls the future: who controls the present controls the past."*
>
> —*1984* by George Orwell

There are facts and then there are alternative facts. Usually, the latter conflicts with the former, but how does that happen? To understand how AI can influence the development of alternative facts, we need to start with a core tenet—motivation.

What is the motivation for someone or an organization to present alternative facts? To be perfectly clear, an alternative fact is not a fact; it is disinformation: the deliberate manipulation of factual information for a deceptive purpose.

In George Orwell's dystopian novel *1984*, we are first introduced to the idea of alternative facts when we learn of Winston Smith, the main protagonist of the story, and his work in the Ministry of Truth. There his job is to constantly rewrite the "truth" of the past, especially when it does not align with other known facts as determined by the authorities. Early in the story, he is directed by the government to rewrite a past fact about the amount of chocolate rations the people of Oceania will receive.

The story of *1984* is a dystopian vision of the year 1984, written by Orwell in 1948. It is about a nation struggling with an unspecified post-war event that leaves its people with meager resources and under the control of a surveillance government. Chocolate rations therefore were a big thing, especially when the government had previously made promises about the amount people would be given. The rewriting of the rations' records by Winston (lowering the amount promised to match the current amount awarded) introduced an *alternative* fact.

People of Oceania may have questioned what they believed was said in the past, but the official records did not align with their memory. It was the systematic destruction of reality and a reminder from Orwell that in our everyday lives we too are fallible when it comes to our memory. The novel introduced readers to the term "doublethink," which required the characters in his novel to accept two often conflicting beliefs as true. When one fact is challenged with an alternative, the people of Oceania do not discard one for the other. They accept both, because not accepting the first real fact and replacing it would be an admission that they were initially wrong.

While this is fictionalized in the novel, there are real-life applications to this lesson. Often people are entrenched in a belief (their first fact), and replacing that belief, even when there is obvious reasoning to do so, is something many of us are reluctant to do. It is unsettling to be wrong about something because if we can be wrong about one thing, then we could be wrong about other things. It is easier to believe we were mostly right about something and seek confirmation without looking at things objectively.

While the story of Winston Smith is a fictional narrative, its influence in our modern culture still resonates. In 2017, a new US President was elected, and he gave his inauguration speech as many did before from the steps of the United States Capitol. The building at one end of the National Mall faces the Washington Monument, and in the space between, people gather to hear the speech. The crowd in 2017 was estimated to be between 300,000 and 600,000 people. The White House stated, "This was the largest audience to ever witness an inauguration—period—both in person and around the globe." But it was not.

Journalists covering the event noted the record-setting crowds of the 2009 inauguration, estimated at 1.8 million people. How could

2017 be larger? The National Park Service, which manages the National Mall, does not provide official numbers of events held on the grounds, but there was other data. First, the number of people using the D.C. Metro subway system was 513,000 in 2009 and 193,000 in 2017, and it is a good proxy for the total number that attended. Second, there was a side-by-side photo comparison of the crowd during the speech taken from the same vantage point atop the Washington Monument. The two photos contrast each other, with the one from 2009 showing the mall filled with people, while the photo from 2017 shows a lot of empty space. Clearly more people attended in 2009.

When asked about the discrepancy between the press secretary's characterization and the evidence, White House counselor Kellyanne Conway said, ". . .our press secretary gave *alternative* facts." The interviewer responded, ". . .alternative facts are not facts. They're falsehoods."

While the interviewer was factually correct, something more important had just occurred. This government was shaping information for its *own narratives*. Unlike during Watergate, when the government was trying to suppress information, removing it from the news cycle, this new administration was openly *adding* information as alternative facts. It was a form of Orwell's doublethink that subtly asks people to simultaneously hold two conflicting pieces of information as truths.

Much of the debate about the inauguration numbers depended on what people would verify from the photos from 2009 and 2017. It was not difficult to fake a single photo. Everyone knew about Photoshop. However, since there were so many photos from independent sources, different news outlets, the National Park Service, and individuals, the photographic evidence was strong.

Back then, manipulating a couple of photos might initially cast doubt on claims of crowd size, but it would be easily defeated when other pictures showed the truth. Now imagine how this changes with AI. Instead of editing a few existing photos individually, a whole new catalog of photos is created. Videos are created using a blend of real photos from the event as inputs. Add video from an in-person perspective of people holding their cell phones, all of it creating authenticity. Imagine you saw ten, or ten thousand, of these alternative-fact-proving pictures and videos, including people talking in the crowd about the astonishing numbers. It would be convincing on a scale nearly impossible before generative AI.

In 2017 you would need hundreds of skilled graphic designers to create a sizable portfolio of false photos. It would cost a lot of money and require time, likely weeks to complete. Time and money are big, often insurmountable, barriers. It is why large-scale disinformation campaigns require the funding of an adversarial government. But in the AI era, the costs are diminished, nearly free, and nearly anyone can provide alternative facts.

Negotiating Truth

We are not different from the people in 1938 listening to *The War of the Worlds*. Think of the woman anxiously turning the dials on her radio or the man panicking while he called the police station. Each was navigating the truth. Our emotions can drive our behavior and cloud our judgment in the moment. What is increasingly apparent is the difference in the way technology plays a role in how we gather and interpret information. Instead of a few radio stations, newspapers, and television broadcasters, AI-driven social media gives us much more. It introduces us to *thousands* of sources and places them in our hands at precisely the right time, something radio and newspapers could never accomplish. Those legacy mediums certainly attempted sensationalism to win over larger audiences, but they were less precise than AI's ability to trigger reactions. We now find ourselves negotiating our emotions and information at the same time.

AI can be finely tuned toward our interests, biases, and even our false beliefs. The echo chamber effect and the volume of noise that are continually testing and retesting us are not just an endless scroll; they are part of an endless experiment.

We understand that the panic of *The War of the Worlds* was manufactured by rivalry between those wanting to control information and validate their place in the information hierarchy. It was a struggle for truth with financial motives, negotiated by whoever controlled the narrative. It was a small and exclusive circle between newspapers and radio. It is a meaningful lesson from the past, repeating itself with one important change: AI has just handed this power to everyone.

Key Takeaways

- *The War of the Worlds* is a story less about a make-believe radio show and more about newspapers fabricating the panic story themselves. The purpose was to discredit radio, which they viewed as a competitive threat to their industry.
- Truth requires verification frameworks. We can establish truth through evidence, logic, observed outcomes, and consensus.
- AI democratizes deception by lowering barriers of cost and content. Creating evidence-based information for newspapers or video for television once required substantial funding, staff, and time. AI nearly eliminates all of these and, when paired with social media, fundamentally changes how we acquire information.

- Negotiating truth now means we are our own truth referees. With institutional trust at historic lows, individuals must actively verify information rather than passively consume it. We must also determine what we can believe in order to make more reliable decisions.

Notes

1. It is important to note that the data supporting the low number of listeners was reported only by the radio trade journal. The data is absent from newspaper reporting, including that of The New York Times. "Press and Public Divided in Reaction to Mars Program," *Broadcasting* 15, no. 10 (1938): 15–28.
2. Rather than "corners," the ancient text likely refers to the four reaches, meaning the cardinal points of the compass. Ancient people considered the rising sun as forward, and eventually words for left, right, and back were translated into the familiar compass directions. Kayle B. De Waal, "Does the Bible Teach that the Earth Is Flat?," Biblical Research Institute, accessed November 20, 2025, `https://adventistbiblicalresearch.org/articles/does-the-bible-teach-that-the-earth-is-flat`

Chapter 3

Open Your Eyes

If You Can Dream It. . .

A dot pulses in the darkness.

A single pixel of light appears alive and insistent. It brightens and fades, and then flares again, cycling through colors from rich red to a vibrant violet several times.

Then it settles.

Soon, another dot ignites beside it. Then another, and another. A cascade of luminous dots, each performing its unique dance. One by one, they connect. Within seconds, there are millions. Millions. Sixteen million dots weave together, self-assembling into a single image. They are guided by a reference and an idea.

To the naked eye, the dance is invisible, with each dot, each calculation of its color and location, occurring at nearly the speed of light. To the machine itself, powered by specialized graphic processors known as GPUs, the task is seemingly effortless. It creates images in a pointillism style reminiscent of a Vincent van Gogh self-portrait, yet when we zoom out, all those pixels are indistinguishable on the screen from those of a photograph. Crisp, clean, perfect.

This is generative AI (GenAI) imagery: fanciful, abstract, and appearing more real than ever before. It is changing how we view and see the world around us. It is also changing our perceptions of what is, in fact, real.

■ ■ ■

Imagine being able to look inside the computer as this process is unfolding and having the ability to watch each dot flutter into creation. Initially, the process and all those dots might appear random. They are not. There are places for certain dots, spaces to be filled, and others to be left alone and empty. As the image takes shape, it gradually begins to reveal itself—its colors, its composition, its subject, and its point of view.

When AI creates an image, it is a bit like an orchestra conductor directing each musician and providing precise timing and cues for their individual part in the music. The conductor nods, and a dot illuminates. Another stare, and the strings brighten. Yet, unlike a music score, which is prewritten, practiced, and performed, AI-generated images are improvised and made anew in the moment, based simply on a description and a reference to many similar items. Prompts like "a kitten playing with a ball of yarn" or "a sunset at the beach" are all AI needs to create a picture. Perhaps instead of a conductor of a well-rehearsed orchestra, what is happening here is more like a jazz ensemble, where the music is structured but less composed until the moment arrives—that is, if jazz ensembles had a director.

A directive for generative AI imagery is the prompt—the text of the idea that gives it meaning and direction. Much like a jazz musician might start a song that reminds them of a moonlight walk in New Orleans or the struggle of a lost love, the prompt is the idea that begins the process.

While an AI image and a new song may be things we have never seen or heard before, they are likely familiar. Those kittens and sunsets resemble others you have seen, as does the new song. This is not luck but, in both cases, a result of a staggering number of practice sessions. The musician might draw from a few hundred songs they learned in the past, while larger AI models will draw on *billions* of images and data they have captured from the Internet.

The AI process is, of course, more complex than *one* computer learning from *one* source. In fact, the latest AI models supporting GenAI use *trillions* of tokens, where a token represents a word, a word part, a phrase, or a group of words. In a nod to the competitiveness of creating these models, platforms have discontinued reporting the size of their datasets; however, the latest models from OpenAI (ChatGPT) are estimated to be trained using 10–13 trillion tokens. Essentially, everything known on the Internet. According to open-source data from `commoncrawl.org`, there are over 250 billion web pages. They also report that 3–5 billion are added each month. It is an incomprehensible amount of information, yet the AI models seem insatiable in their desire to use it—so much so that the AI industry is starting to be concerned that it is running out of available training data.

What does all this mean? A vast amount of data is being consumed by a handful of AI platform providers, and there seems to be no end to their appetite for information. A billion or a trillion—either number seems inconceivable, so suffice it to say that they use a *lot* of data. So, what can they really do once they have taken in that much information?

Natural-Born Instincts

"Well, who you gonna believe? Me or your own eyes?"

—Chico Marx, *Duck Soup*

Part of being a successful species requires humans to have some higher-functioning capabilities. These are the types of capabilities that help us identify a dangerous berry from one that is safe, a predator from prey, and that sense we get from a light breeze that a storm is coming. This sense of safety from harm is the same mechanism we employ to identify misinformation and separate fact from fiction. We have natural-born instincts that evolved to enable us to survive dangerous situations. However, these are also the same processes that are being exploited by AI.

Like all animals, our brains have dedicated systems for sight and sound. Many of those systems have a hardwired-like connection between the sensory input (e.g., your eyes) and the operating portion of the brain. That is, there are dedicated parts of our brain like the occipital lobe for sight and the temporal lobe for sound. Humans and animals have made similar adaptions. For example, eagles have a much better sense of sight due to their adaptation for hunting. In their retina, they have nearly three times the number of sensitive cells that respond to light and color. This gives them the ability to see prey from up to two miles away.[1]

What makes humans better is not the hardwiring of the sensory inputs; it is the processing of that information from multiple systems into higher-level thinking. The functional part of our brain can use the input from two eyes to sense the depth and color of an object. Although many animals can accomplish the same, a differentiator is how we process that information and tap into our working memory in our prefrontal cortex. The prefrontal cortex also participates in a variety of higher cognitive functions such as planning, reasoning, thinking, and decision-making. Humans do this far better than any other animal, and regarding vision, it gives us the ability to match images we see with things we have seen before. It also gives us the ability to see something and process the information afterward.

Research has shown that we can do this at astonishing speeds. A study by MIT neuroscientists found that participants could identify characteristics of an image that had been shown to them for only 13 and 80 milliseconds (there are 1000 milliseconds in 1 second). Our unique capability to couple information from multiple input sensors (sight, sound, touch) and then process it as a cohesive output is the synergy that helps us detect and interpret information.

While detecting false information is an evolutionary survival skill, it is increasingly becoming an AI survival skill. Recall that the early versions of AI text-to-image creators such as DALL-E, Midjourney, and Adobe Firefly were introduced to the public in late 2022 and early 2023. Their results were stunning by comparison to the previous time-consuming and skill-intensive efforts of Photoshop, but far from perfect. However, by 2025, researchers with Universitat Autònoma de Barcelona found that participants struggled even then to differentiate between AI-generated and human-generated pictures. Nearly 40% of AI-generated images were misidentified as real (human-generated).[2]

If you were an early adopter of these tools, you may remember that images of people tended to be out-of-this-worldly perfect and often out of context. Asking for a picture of "a man sitting on a bench in the fall" would more likely look like a professional model posing for an L.L. Bean advertisement than something you might just see while running in the park. If it were possible to create pictures that were too idyllic, then that would be an appropriate description of that time. The AI image tools continue to get better, and until we reach the end of the AI equivalent of Moore's law, they will exponentially improve.

Other research also suggested that humans have an innate ability to detect fake images of *people* more easily than fake images of landscapes or buildings. This may be because our evolution as social creatures makes us more sensitive to differentiating between (safe) people.[3]

While a picture can be worth a thousand words, it can also be worth a lot more in terms of credibility. Imagine you saw a plaintext meme on your social media feed that read, "President Declares War after bombs explode," or "JFK Jr. Is Still Alive Farming in Iowa."

You might simply scroll past it without any thought. Just another square black box with white text and little relevance. A meme about JFK Jr., who died in 1999, is hardly relevant. The other, about a bomb, might make some of us pause, but there are a lot of "news" items in your feed, and you likely choose to keep scrolling. That is, if you read them at all.

In the seemingly endless feeds of social media, where we spend an average of 147 minutes daily, we have almost too many choices for information.[4] Researchers refer to this as *high-choice environments*, and they can overload our senses and disrupt how we process information. As a result, we use mental shortcuts—our mind's heuristics—to filter or accept information. For example, plaintext memes get quickly shuffled to the background. But what happens when those memes have accompanying pictures? There are an estimated 3.2 billion images shared online *daily*; millions flow into Facebook, Instagram, and X, plus millions more onto the traditional news platforms. Part of the reason for all these images is that they capture our attention in ways that words alone simply cannot. Sometimes those pictures are useful for the narrative, or they are simply used to disrupt your processing of information, and they generally fall into five categories. See Table 3.1 for a breakdown of these categories and their familiar use in social media.[5]

Table 3.1 Five Purposes for Photos Used in Social Media

Image Purpose	Description
Window dressing	An eye-catching and engaging picture that is unrelated to the text. Real or AI-generated.
Informative	Real photos that provide evidence supporting the text. The truth.

Image Purpose	Description
Misinformation	Real photos used out of context. Example: a picture of an angry protester during a peaceful public demonstration.
Disinformation	Real or AI-generated photos purposefully used to provide false and misleading evidence. Negative intent.
Repurposed	Real photos from another time or place that are similar to the text's claim of truth. They provide "evidence" somewhere between misinformation (misunderstanding or lacking context) and disinformation, depending on the creator's either naïve or malicious intent.

Picture This

When you see an online posting with an accompanying photo that seems disconnected, and you find yourself asking why this picture is here, well, the answer is "window dressing." The photos, not the words, are attempting to disrupt and capture your attention. Think about cat videos and puppy dogs in advertising.[6] Or a selfie on LinkedIn unrelated to the text of the post. The latter is an example of breaking the easy association in our minds of the picture and the meaning of the post. The incongruence of the two is purposely used to pause your automatic processing of the information, pause the scroll, and forces you to spend slightly more time trying to understand the connection between the image and the words.

Confirmation bias, the instinct that let our ancestors more easily accept a cave painting as proof, also has a lesser-known cousin called the "truthiness effect." When we see a photo, it can significantly influence our perception of the truth. Again, the familiar phrase about a picture being worth a thousand words has some truth of its own. When we read something along with a picture, our mind relies on a mechanism called *cognitive processing fluency*. As we see the picture, we also "picture it" in our mind more easily (fluently) than we would if we were interpreting the written text describing the same scene. The picture *eases* our understanding of what is written, and we do not need that additional micro-moment of extra mental capacity to draw it on our own. The brain misinterprets the fluency of processing information as truth. Otherwise, we would need to picture in our mind an alternative view that is untrue. We are capable of this, of course, but in those brief and overwhelming views of the meme with a picture, we simply accept it as true. Things that are plausible and simple to understand can stay under the radar of our own doubts.

Informative pictures can have the same mental effect, especially when they are well-intentioned. These are the best examples of the truth visually. Not surprisingly, you will see these in accredited academic forums and traditional established news organizations. In contrast, real photos used unintentionally or out of context with the message contribute to misinformation.

Consider when the purpose is to deceive a viewer. When the writer is deliberately changing the narrative away from the truth, using images common in propaganda, then they are creating disinformation.

Repurposed images often fall between misinformation and disinformation. They could be providing truthful information, or they could be a real image positioned to tell a completely different narrative. Either way, all images, still or video, follow those same mechanisms in our brain. What is fascinating is that the ease of our mind's understanding of what we see significantly contributes to its believability. As the capabilities of AI continue to improve, its tools will provide images that just "make sense" rather than ones that might make you stop for a moment and question their authenticity.

Images can be useful to convey truth or sow doubts. In addition to increasing the truthiness, eye-tracking studies show that information with accompanying images also holds our attention longer and increases the likelihood of its being shared with others online. But this can also be impacted by the context of the information. If you are familiar with a topic, you are less likely to accept an alternative belief about it. For example, the claim that JFK Jr. is still alive is less believable to people who follow the Kennedy family history. For people who do not, the research also showed some unexpected results.

When participants are given a statement about a little-known celebrity who is still alive along with their picture, they believe it. It seems simple. However, in the same experiment with the same photo, but the opposite statement (that this person is not alive), they also believed it. While the photo in each example did not provide any evidence on its own about whether the person was dead or alive, what did occur is that they most easily accepted the truthiness of the statement compared to other participants who were not shown photos. The photos themselves gave credibility to either claim.

Researchers repeated this experiment with other claims about the quality of a bottle of wine along with a photo of a quill pen dipped in an ink well. Another noted that giraffes were the only mammals that cannot jump, accompanied by a close-up shot of a giraffe's face (not their jumping or nonjumping legs).[7] In all cases, the truthiness effect persisted. The photos added no evidence for the truth of the statement, yet they provided confidence to the participants.

While "window dressing" photos build confidence, "informative" photos that provide supporting evidence increase confidence even more. Why does this matter? In the real world, finding a photo of something that is untrue is difficult. At best, a manipulative person might use another photo taken out of context as proof of their false statement. In the world of advancing GenAI technology, however, the barriers to finding the perfect (fake) photo are drastically reduced. And the fact that our mind can be *warmed up*, simply primed, to the idea of accepting something as true when given a picture or video has profound implications for our unguarded society and the prevalence of misinformation.

The cognitive processes associated with trust go beyond photos alone. The integration of realistic video and generative speech also gives synthetic materials a human-likeness that builds trust.[8] The introduction of a more advanced version of SORA by OpenAI and Google's VEO 3, introduced in 2025, was a significant milestone. Not only did these video-generation models improve the quality of the images they created from text prompts, but, importantly, they added sound and *voice*. Anthropomorphism is that human-likeness we experience from machines that enhances the perceived humanness of AI, like your conversations with ChatGPT and your experiences with AI-generated video. Combining familiar audio along with visual information again works with our natural-born instincts to trust what we can see and now hear. Realistically animating the picture raises the possibility it is real. Easing meaning and content into our consciousness in this manner becomes more fluid, acceptable, when we are not struggling to understand the medium of the messages. As we spend less mental energy on thinking about the images we are seeing, we tend to also expend less on questioning the message itself.

Our ability to view images and match them to our memory of similar images from the past is one way we validate something as real, since it preexisted in our memories. Show someone a picture of an ice cream cone, and they match it to one they held in their hand before. This creates confidence that the image is actually an ice cream cone. We now know AI creates images that are visually similar to reality, but our prior experiences, like holding the ice cream cone in your hand, can also be a tool to detect false images. Where were you when you were with the ice cream cone? What was the setting? The time of year? Was that time of the day or the time of year appropriate for the scene? What was the expression on the faces of people around you (usually happy)? Our real human experiences contribute to our ability to determine the authenticity of images where context and meaning matter.

These details are more difficult for AI to create, since AI systems do not understand circumstances or how emotions can relate to a photo. However, guided by a human, those emotional gaps can be overcome with the skills of an AI specialist. In other words, simple compositions created without much consideration can contain more flaws than those revised repeatedly to get a better result. People with nefarious intentions, like scam artists, are the ones who will work harder to create deceptive information. Someone who is harmlessly suggesting that it would be fun to go grab some ice cream will just take the first thing AI creates and send it to you. Your ability to match pictures to your memories seems like a great way to avoid being misled by AI. But how good is your memory?

I Do Recall

"We met at nine.
We met at eight.
I was on time.
No, you were late.
Ah yes! I remember it well."

—Alan Jay Lerner, *Gigi: A Musical Play*[9]

Think of a good memory you have from long in the past. Do you recall how you felt in that moment, and are you certain of the details? The emotions, the imagery, and the data are all encapsulated in your specific memories. Do other people who shared that event with you remember it in *exactly* the same way? It is an easy experiment to try and likely when working together you and your friends will remember more details about the past than you would simply on your own. You both store and recall parts of a shared experience differently, not by dubious selection of what you want to remember, but because how we store information inconsistently.

Data professionals might draw the analogy that storing and recalling your memories is the same as a computer using a hard drive. However, our memories are not stored like digital recordings. Instead, our memories are stored in fragments of our experiences. The visuals, sounds, emotions, and our interpretation are encoded across different regions of our brain. When needed, our prefrontal cortex helps retrieve the information, but it is not pure data-in and data-out. We shape those memories, adding small parts of detail that suit us and sometimes removing, choosing not to store, those parts that trouble us. This is the fallibility of human memories.

When you ask someone to recall the famous line from *Star Wars: The Empire Strikes Back* where Darth Vader reveals he is Luke's father, most people get it wrong. We remember the gist of the scene between Luke and Darth Vader, but misremember the line as "*Luke*, I am your father," rather than the correct line, "No, I am your father." The context is that he is speaking to Luke, and changing the phrase fits. In addition, the repeated misquoting of the line can also contribute to how we remember hearing it. The latter is what marketing experts rely on when relentlessly repeating product claims such that they become embedded in your recall. Or how a song can win you over after it has been played again and again. The repetition of information gives us the confidence that the false association is real, in what psychologists call the *illusory truth effect.*

The illusory truth effect works on the power of reinforcing ideas and is frequently used to spread unfounded statements (think of statements by politicians), misinformation, and disinformation. Since repetition is the key mechanism, social media, which has built-in hyper capabilities for sharing information, is especially prone to this type of truth-decaying influence.

That memory you have from years ago may elicit vivid emotions—hopefully ones that make you smile and remember the event fondly. The details surrounding the memory may be more vague. Fortunately, we have social media rituals like Throwback Thursday, when your friends might dig up old photos and repost them for you. What would we do without friends like this? Well, there is an algorithm for that too, and you have likely seen it on Facebook with the "remember when" photo montages. For a more analog approach to recalling your memories, you might reference old photos, letters, cards, and diaries. All these artifacts, whether in digital or hard copy, help fill in the details of our memories.

When social media platforms nudge your memories by recalling older posts and photos, they are not just providing you with a nice tool to remember your past events; they are actively encouraging you to repost them to your friends. Why? The answer is that Facebook's motivation is about engagement, not supporting your memories, but those photos do help. They help so much that psychologist Qi Wang has suggested that social media contributes to the fallibility of our memories.

We use the Internet and social media as tools to offload the mental burden of remembering things. We remember *where* to look up those adorable pictures of our children playing at the beach and commit less of the details to our real memory. Researchers also refer to this as the *Google effect* since it is not limited to our visual memories. It is much like how I am writing this paragraph and thinking more about the ideas I want to share than the spelling of each word, since I have spellcheck built into my computer to handle that task. Our mind works the same way. It is not lazy per se, but efficient, and when it perceives a mental shortcut (heuristics), we tend to follow it so we can focus more on other things.

What does the Google effect mean for our ability to recall images, facts, and other information? What is the impact of recalling these details when what we find during the retrieval process is different because of an exhausting amount of AI-generated misinformation? (A bigger question here is how can we possibly use the Internet to recall only *verifiable* information and nothing else?) It means we are less likely to commit details to our memories that are less useful to us when we need to recall them. For example, if you are of a certain age that predated the adoption of cell phones and saved contacts, you might have a better ability to remember people's phone numbers. Before a person's number could be easily stored on your device, you *needed* to store that information yourself. When someone asked what your phone number was or the phone number of your brother, it was easy for you to recall. Today, it would be rare for someone to be able to recall the phone numbers of their 10 closest friends and family without needing to look them up. We delegate this task to technology.

We can agree that we still can remember phone numbers, but perhaps we are losing those abilities to easier technology as we practice them less. Consider trying to remember a long number. Look at the following number for 10 seconds, then look away and try to recall it exactly:

91 562 222 6431

How did you do? If our memories worked like digital recorders, this would be an easy task, but it is not.

Now look at the number grouped in a different way:

91 562 222 6431

You should be able to recall parts of this number more easily, which is exactly why phone numbers and other identifying numbers are presented in smaller groupings of three to four numbers. We can remember several smaller groups of numbers better than one large number because of how our mind groups information, much like data packets.

However, as the task of what we remember grows more complex, like an entire event with more details, this becomes more difficult. The information is less objective, like a number, and requires more interpretation before it can be encoded and stored in our memory. For example, think of a memory of your family standing in front of a building while on vacation overseas. Your focus is on the people and less on the details of the building and its surroundings. Later you can recall and remember them vividly, but what about the background? Did the building have many windows, and how tall was it? What about the other people? Since it was in a foreign place, your memory may be that the people were like others from that country—our mind can fill in the gaps when we recall the information, even when it might not be right. Asked to draw this memory on a sheet of paper, we would not produce a photographic replica.

Aside from our drawing skills, we would miss or create information we did not originally see. Furthermore, the intensity of the memory does not improve its recall. One might assume that traumatic or highly emotional memories are "locked in" with more detail.

We might feel this is true too as we recall where we were on 9/11 or our *vivid* memories at a family member's wedding. Our emotions, fear or happiness, can play a role in our recall of information, which is where bias can be introduced.

Noise and Judgment

On a practical level, we develop *noise* in our memories in what could be described as confusion and a mixing up of the objective evidence. How is this possible? The fallibility of our memory is in part the fallibility of the biological design of our brain. With different parts of the brain tasked with processing different sensory inputs, where and how we store information can get muddled. We do not operate like a computer or AI, yet we are increasingly relying on AI for verifiable information.

Researchers such as Martin Hilbert suggest many of the common cognitive biases that impact most decisions are a result of the fallibility of our minds to correctly store information. It is a different type of "noise" than we have been discussing. The noise that Hilbert refers to is the noise of how we tend to mix up and confuse some (usually small) details. We tend to be vulnerable to our older memories and build assumptions that seep into the current ones.

A good example of this is confirmation bias and stereotypes we might have about other people. Hilbert shares an example where most people report that they are better than average at driving. Yet we all have the same evidence from our driving experiences that for most of us should objectively tell us we are just average. We overestimate our ability as we recall our memory of our good driving and overemphasize those rare times we witness a poor driver. Our assessment and our judgment are impacted by the noise of what we remember, of what we can recall, and even how we can incorrectly process information in the moment.

Hilbert is not suggesting we get it wrong all the time, only that we might not always get it right. And in that gap, between what happened and what we remember happening, something familiar is at work.

Think back to that first dot, pulsing alone in the dark. Others join it, each not placed at random, but referencing an idea, a prompt, a pattern the machine has seen before. The result was not a perfect recall of an image, it was a creation assembled to match expectation.

Your brain does the same thing every time it reaches for a memory. There is no file retrieval system, no replay, only fragments, instinct, and references working in real time to smooth the misremembered parts, brightening a face, filling in the perfect sunset. Close to accurate, yet not quite true.

It is not only memory. The same type of mechanism is at work every time you search for an answer. Type a symptom into a search bar at 2 a.m. and the result that loads first, reads easiest, and matches what you already fear will feel more true than the one a specialist might point to. Look up a historical event you vaguely recall from school and the version that confirmed what you learned, what you thought you learned, will feel more true than the one that complicates it. Searching for truth, in a photo, a memory, a medical question, a piece of history, runs on the same fuel. Not evidence or accuracy, but ease of belief.

None of this requires artificial intelligence. Our minds have been improvising since long before anyone coined the term GenAI, and where we didn't need to improvise, we sought truth among a record, a source, something beyond our own knowledge. What is changing is information itself and who creates it. Every photo you have paused on, every shared meme, every document you have taken at face value, every search you have run at midnight, every story you endlessly followed on your news feed, all of these have been quietly learning, working toward something else: the version of truth your mind is most likely to accept.

Key Takeaways

- Our human vulnerability to misinformation is not a character flaw; it is biology. Those same instincts and mental shortcuts our ancestors relied upon as hunter-gatherers now work against us in an environment saturated with information. Recognizing our limitations can guide better responses to AI-triggered misinformation.
- AI misinformation and disinformation work best at the fringes of believability. Mixing true information with some misinformation lowers our barriers of disbelief.
- Memory and perceptions are not recordings; they are reconstructions built from the moments, fragments, and expectations we have from the past and are similar to the mechanism that GenAI uses to create images from a prompt and pixels. Neither is always true.
- We have long checked our fallible memories against something beyond our own mind—an old photo collection, a research document, a search result. That outside evidence is increasingly produced by the same systems that exploit gaps in our biases.

Notes

1. Eagles' visual adaptation is so specialized for daytime hunting that they have a diminished ability to see at night compared to humans.
   Lidia V. Zueva, Vladimir I. Makarov, Astrid Zayas-Santiago, Tatiana B. Golubeva, Elena Korneeva, Alexey Savvinov, Misty J. Eaton, Serguei N Skatchkov, and Mikhail Inyushin "Müller Cell Alignment in Bird Fovea: Possible Role in Vision." *Journal of Neuroscience and Neuroengineering* 3, no. 2 (2014): 85–91. `https://doi.org/10.1166/jnsne.2014.1104`

2. Daniela Velásquez-Salamanca, Miguel Ángel Martín-Pascual, and Celia Andreu-Sánchez, "Interpretation of AI-Generated vs. Human-Made Images," *Journal of Imaging* 11, no. 7 (2025): 227. https://doi.org/10.3390/jimaging11070227
3. While the research shows people are better at identifying faces compared to pictures of objects and landscapes, the results overall were only marginally better than 50/50 random at 65%.
   Thomas Roca, Anthony Cintron Roman, Jehú Torres Vega, Marcelo Duarte, Pengce Wang, Kevin White, Amit Misra, Juan Lavista Ferres "How Good Are Humans at Detecting AI-Generated Images? Learnings from an Experiment." *arXiv* (2025). https://doi.org/10.48550/arXiv.2507.18640
4. The metrics for time spent online by platform are elusive. While most companies like Facebook are quick to note the number of active users, which doubled from 2015 (1.59 billion) to 2025 (3.07 billion), they do not report details about time spent online. This is of keen interest to advertisers, and it is only anecdotally mentioned by companies. The estimates for time online are provided by multiple sources with similar results, including Brandwatch (https://www.brandwatch.com/blog/amazing-social-media-statistics-and-facts).
5. Adapted from Eryn J. Newman and Norbert Schwarz, "Misinformed by Images: How Images Influence Perceptions of Truth and What Can Be Done about It," *Current Opinion in Psychology* 56 (2024), https://doi.org/10.1016/j.copsyc.2023.101778
6. Animals have long been used in advertising to trigger nurturing and emotional responses associated with consumer products. An early example includes Nipper, the terrier dog mascot for the Victor-Victrola Talking Machines, later RCA's record players. In modern times, we frequently see dogs used for products unrelated to animals, such as Bullseye, the dog pitching products for Target stores. Dogs are featured more often since they provide a higher consumer empathy response compared to cats.
   Lei Jia, Xiaojing Yang, and Yuwej Jiang, "The Pet Exposure Effect: Exploring the Differential Impact of Dogs versus Cats on Consumer Mindsets," *Journal of Marketing* 86, no. 5 (2022): 42–57, https://doi.org/10.1177/00222429221078036

7. Readers might pause reading this statement. Although seemingly unnatural for an animal with the proportions of a giraffe, they can indeed jump as high as six feet. "Giraffe," SeaWorld Parks and Entertainment, `https://seaworld.org/animals/facts/mammals/giraffe`
8. Ilaria Torre, Jeremy Goslin, and Laurence White, "If Your Device Could Smile: People Trust Happy-Sounding Artificial Agents More," *Computers in Human Behavior* 105 (2020): 106215, `https://doi.org/10.1016/j.chb.2019.106215`
9. Alan Jay Lerner, "I Remember It Well," in *Gigi: A Musical Play* (New York: Random House, 1959).

Chapter 4

Can a Computer Know Your Vulnerability?

Emotional Algorithms

Imagine for a moment that you are the lead data scientist for a spy agency tasked with gathering information about specific people of interest. Your duty is surveillance, and as the word implies, you need to learn as much about your target as possible . . . without them knowing they are being tracked. In your covert approach, you need to learn their demographic details (name, location, occupation, etc.) along with any vices or vulnerabilities they may possess that could be used, if needed, to leverage a conversation or motivate your target toward a particular decision.

All of this seems very possible even with the most basic of technology, and you could assemble a brief profile of a few pages of information and pictures of your target, their family, and friends. As you present this to your boss, proud of your accomplishment, instead of rewarding a job well done, they expand the scope of your task. Instead of tracking just one target, they want you to track all their friends and all the friends of their friends. They want the profiles to go deeper—not just a few pages of cursory information, but *hundreds* of pages of information to summarize the *thousands* of things that can be known about an individual.

What would it take to target half of the adult U.S. population in this much detail? To create a profile for just one person, an experienced agent requires about 100 hours of work, about 2–3 weeks. Now, multiply that by 135 million people over the age of 18, and you have 13.5 billion hours of work. With 100,000 field agents, it would still take 68 *years* to complete the task, at which point most of the targeted people would have died. An impossible task.

Here is what you do instead. The answer, it turns out, is not hiring 100,000 field agents. It is building a system, an app, that makes people *willingly* provide all that information themselves.

Concern or Legitimate Risk?

And what you do is exactly what the 118th United States Congress feared in 2024 that TikTok, owned by its Chinese parent company, ByteDance, might be doing. The app, with all its engaging videos, was seen as a surveillance tool that knew more about *you* than your closest friends: your emotional triggers, your fears, your political leanings, even your vulnerable moments at 2 a.m. when you open TikTok because you could not sleep. TikTok reported in 2023 that 150 million people in the United States are regular users of the app, which is a significant portion of the 291 million people in the United States over the age of 13. The age of 13 is the limit TikTok imposes on users, and maybe this is specifically where the story of TikTok and the US government begins.

Before the social media app was rebranded as TikTok, it was known as `Musical.ly`, which was started by friends Alex Zhu and Luyu Yang in 2014 and based in Shanghai, China. Its initial focus was on creating short lip-sync videos that users posted online. ByteDance acquired `Musical.ly` in 2017, merging elements of its Douyin short video app into it. Douyin is a similar, separate app exclusively for China, while the rest of the globe uses TikTok, which is available in 150 countries.

Notably, China has stricter content limits and regulation of social media, including age restrictions. In 2019, Douyin limited young people to 40 minutes per day and allowed them to use the app only between 6 a.m. and 10 p.m. The app also required age authentication and parental approval rather than simply self-reporting their age. However, TikTok was less limiting and already under scrutiny in the United States by the Federal Trade Commission (FTC).

In 2019 the FTC fined TikTok and ByteDance what was then a record amount of $5.7 million for collecting information from children under 13 , including their name, email, and location, in violation of the Children's Online Privacy Protection Act (COPPA).[1] It is difficult to determine if the data collection was intentional or a default of their system to collect as much information about users as possible, but it certainly got the unsavory attention of lawmakers.

Another contribution to the story was a pair of laws enacted in China in 2017 requiring Chinese companies to share data: the National Intelligence Law and the Cybersecurity Law. The former states that "all organizations and citizens shall support, assist, and cooperate with national intelligence efforts." In effect, if the government needed data from companies within the country, then these companies would be required to provide it. Despite some similarities to how law enforcement operates in the United States, this was seen as a partnership between the government of China and a company collecting data on people in the United States. Although the CEO of the company explicitly denied that this had ever happened while testifying before a congressional hearing, it was the possibility that lingered.

A series of presidential executive orders specifically aimed at TikTok eventually resulted in the passage of a broader law that included any foreign-controlled social media application, known as the Protecting Americans from Foreign Adversary Controlled Applications Act. The Act grants the president the authority to ban any social media application deemed to be a national security threat.

As of this writing, TikTok has been the only platform subject to this ruling, and the result was to change control such that it is majority-owned by a US company, with data stored on U.S. based servers. It is also banned from all government devices.

Fear, concern, or legitimate risk? Aside from four employees who looked at data about journalists, there are no documented cases of data being misused by TikTok. What motivated the action was the possibility that it could happen. The emotional response, ironically, is a cornerstone of online social media engagement.

The concerns of the US Congress were not entirely about foreign governments looking through your virtual window to spy on you, but rather about the fear that the information they gathered about you might be used to exploit individuals or spread propaganda that served their interests. And while it sounds like science fiction, there is some reality, at least in the science part.

Signals

Sara did not tell anyone about the breakup—not her parents, not her coworkers, not even her friends. On a Sunday afternoon in May, after years together, she and Jonathan decided to end things. They had been growing apart for a while, spending less time together as they noticed their interests and paths in life were gradually moving in different directions. It was no surprise to either of them, yet it felt uncomfortable. A major chapter in each of their lives was closing, and at the moment they wanted to deal with it privately.

A few days passed before Sara noticed. First on Instagram, then on TikTok. What she saw in her feed was changing. Not because of anything she posted. That was the last thing she wanted to do right now, and neither had Jonathan. Yet, she was seeing videos about recovering from long relationships and ads for solo vacation packages. The algorithms feeding her social media did not just know from the data she posted; they deduced it from her behavior.

Recently she had been posting fewer photos; as we all know, we only really post our happy moments, and those were fleeting in recent times. Her location data, captured by her phone and shared with the social media platforms, showed she and Jonathan were spending less time together in the same places. Her late-night scrolling patterns changed, both the hour of the day and the time spent looking at melancholy content. Her Spotify song choices changed. Maybe it was time for other changes too.

She searched online for a new job and Googled "how to break a lease." None of these data points by themselves would announce that she was going through a breakup, but together they showed the algorithms a truth about her. Before she shared the news with another human, a computer had figured it out. Maybe it knew the relationship was not going to work even before she did.

The story of Sara and Jonathan is a composite of real-life experiences and real data that many of you might find relatable. The notion that AI is *listening* to me is a commonly reported feeling people have about AI, along with the fear of surveillance. Forty-five percent of people in the United States believe their devices are likely eavesdropping before showing them product advertisements.[2]

While social media platforms state this is not occurring and would be a violation of public trust, they underscore that what AI is really good at is recognizing patterns. Like Sara, our behavioral patterns change and can be a proxy for life events.

A study of a million online Reddit posts shows our language, the words and tone, changes about three months before a relationship breakup. Further, Facebook and researchers at Cornell University published a paper about the development of an algorithm that can accurately guess who your partner is (and who is not). Using the "dispersion rate" among your social circles, they can predict whether you will break up based on your connections to your Facebook friends. It may not be absolute, but there are enough markers in your data for social media to home in on to place their bets on targeted advertising.

If our behavior changes before, during, and after a breakup, it creates signals. Just like your best friend might know when something is not right, these signals are measurable data that an algorithm can pick up on. It can do more than guess; it can *infer* from the collective data. The data we (mostly) willfully share with the platforms. Platforms analyze this data using the perfect mechanism, the algorithm, something that was impossible 20 years ago.

Meta and its collection of apps like Facebook and Instagram are running a surveillance system, not for an international spy agency, but for advertisers. Targeted ads form the majority of their business and accounted for 97% of Meta's revenue, which in 2025 was $196 billion. But how exactly do online platforms make all this work?

Personalization Engines

The science of social media algorithms is as closely guarded a trade secret as the legendary Coca-Cola formula. Except the difference is that instead of a static recipe that is nearly 140 years old, the methods companies use to collect data and target you online can change daily. Yesterday's method used to engage you on a social media site can be different from today's or tomorrow's, but there are some fundamentals of online personalization that will not change with the evolving technology. The frequent changes in the algorithm are in response to the changing inputs it receives from you. All those "likes" and "shares" can guide you to new content. Your personal tastes, popular trends, and community interests can quickly change, and as they do, so do the algorithmic selection methods.

Social media has become the information infrastructure, filling the vacuum left by the decline traditional sources. In the United States, about half of adults use Facebook and YouTube *daily*. Other popular platforms include Instagram, TikTok, WhatsApp, Reddit, and X/Twitter, all of which have millions of routine users, and as a result, they have collectively become sources of both entertainment and information. While each has its own approach to displaying content and maximizing revenue, most share some fundamental similarities in how they collect data about you, organize it to create a profile, and use this to show you the most relevant and engaging content.

Some platforms publish high-level explanations of their selection algorithms, such as TikTok, which describes a system of recommendations that aligns users with other users who have similar video patterns and profiles. If you like videos from people with similar interests, then you will be shown similar videos. It is generalized without showing the math, while X/Twitter has a more technical description of its methods, including posting open-source code on GitHub.[3] Shielded in intellectual property secrecy, most other platforms' algorithms are only documented by third parties. These include marketing firms, influencer coaches, and algorithm researchers who are, at best, inferring the mechanics of the recommendation engines based on observations.

To understand how these systems know what they know about you, it helps to see the full picture of the type of data they are actually collecting, and why.

1. **Explicit data:** Information you intentionally share. The data in your profile such as your name, birthday (age), where you live, work, schools attended, relationship status, etc. These are the starting points. Next is what you post. Those adorable photos of your kids at the beach. Your friends and spouse at memorable events. Comments you add to those pictures,

along with comments you make on other posts in your feed. Text of your in-app chats and direct messages.

2. **Third-party data:** Information from data brokers aggregated from public records or gathered from other sources that share data with data brokers.
3. **Behavioral data:** What you do when you are online using the app. Media you engage with, including video and photos, beyond just comments. Your "dwell time" is measured when you look at a video, even in passing. How long you linger on a piece of content tells the algorithms more than you could by adding a deliberate comment. It signals that you were at least curious about its content. They will test this again later with similar content to reaffirm that it was not a mistake. Did you really like it, or was the pause accidental, as though you were interrupted by something else? Test and test again. The algorithm will refine what it knows about you and what you like.
4. **Relational data:** Connections established through your follower and following relationships. Your linkages to your friends and family help build a model, known as a social graph, of your digital community.
5. **Contextual data:** When, where, and how you engage with the application. Includes your device information (e.g., type and model of phone), geographic location, and your connection's IP address and internet service provider.
6. **Inferred data:** Information that is deduced from all the other information. Personality traits, political affiliations, social groups and interests, charitable-giving inclinations, and possible vulnerabilities (e.g., gambling, allergies, fears).

The data you share and the data platforms assemble from other sources are combined to create your digital profile. Everything from your age, income, likes, and dislikes creates a description of you that can be aligned with their content. But to make it useful for providers, it needs a set of rules.

Algorithms are like recipes that provide those rules. Follow the rules and you will make something, like bread. While there are many variations, the basic ingredients remain the same. Your bread recipe needs flour, water, and yeast. An algorithm needs the data described above. Mix it the right way, following the recipe, and it results in a consistent result, whether it is bread or a product advertisement like you might see while browsing online at Amazon, Target, or any other retailer. They all use a variation of these recipes to find the product you are most likely to buy. But it is not a random bet.

Social media sites and online retailers are similar in that they need to decide what to show you that will get your engagement, either in content or in prompting you to purchase a product. They cannot show you everything, so how do they decide? There are distinct steps, from collecting signals about your interests to evaluating the success of their recommendations at the end. Figure 4.1 depicts this typical process flow.

While these steps may be familiar to those who routinely work with data, it is important to note not just the mechanisms, but also the outcomes. The workflow sets in motion a process that can yield unexpected results. It is why everyone sees a different set of posts, videos, or ads.

1. **Signals.** Platforms are continuously collecting your explicit and implicit signals, which are the data they know about you, in addition to the preferences you "signal" through your interactions with the application.

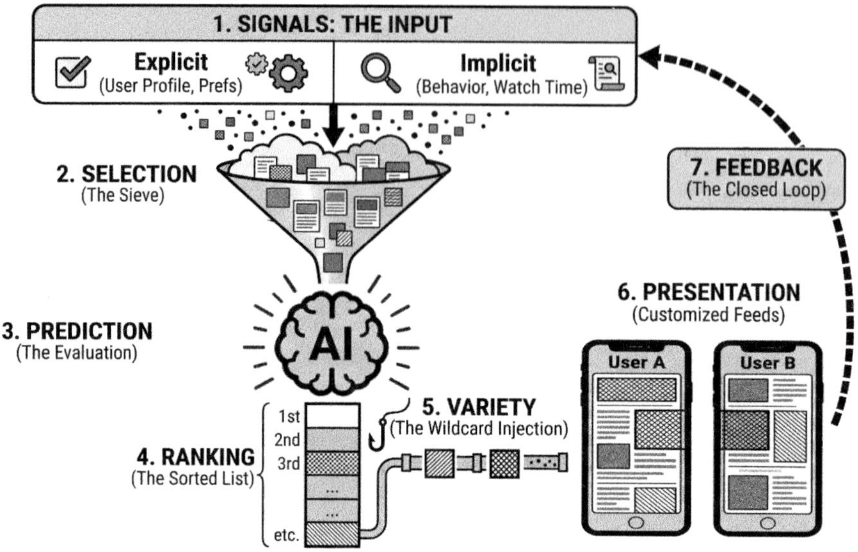

Figure 4.1 Targeted algorithm workflow

2. **Selection.** Using your personal signals, the system builds a subset of content to show you. X/Twitter might select the most current discussion posts on a topic you frequently read. TikTok may choose a list of videos that grabbed your attention recently. This subset may contain thousands of candidates. X/Twitter has reported that when you first log in, it immediately preselects about 1,500 posts.
3. **Prediction.** Given the subset of selected content, the algorithm begins predicting the probability of how you will respond to each piece of content. Whether you click to read, watch a video to completion, write a comment, share, or click "buy" is among the many user actions that it is evaluating.
4. **Ranking.** Depending on the strategic goals of the platform, the previous prediction step scores and ranks the content. A retail site might prioritize the probability of a purchase, while

a social media site could rank content higher based on the likelihood that users will share.

5. **Variety.** Without variety of content in the "For You Feed," the platform risks repetitive content and disengagement, especially when your interests change over time. The algorithm needs to find a way to explore. Maybe you have had a life event, like a new job, relationship, marriage, or moving to a new city. If you have not updated your explicit profile data with this information, then the algorithm will fail to show you new content that aligns with those changes. The variety component is a useful tool to avoid showing you the same old nonrelevant content or content you have previously seen. It also explains why you might see something totally unexpected. It is fishing for data to enhance your profile. It is also how the platform can discover information about you that others do not yet know. Without continuing to experiment with additional content, they may miss finding those additional interests of yours, reducing future revenue opportunities.
6. **Presentation**. In this stage, the ranked content is displayed. It is customized for each user. Two users with similar online communities and following similar people or belonging to similar interest groups often see overlapping, yet distinct, content. No two "For You Feeds" on any platform are the same.
7. **Feedback.** The final step is an evaluation of the outcome of the preceding steps. How successful were the probabilities of the predicted outcomes? The numerical results, the hits and misses, factor into the next cycle of curating content for users. High-performing content is shown to more users with similar "signals." Conversely, low-performing content is pushed lower in the rankings.

All this happens in an instant without the user noticing. The processes are continuously evaluating the available content and your interests. Algorithmic models measure probabilities and adjust the weight they assign to the data variables as they optimize. The objectives are to improve the time users spend on the app, including session depth, predictability, and emotional engagement, which drives repeat use. Truth, balanced viewpoints, and information quality are *secondary* goals compared with engagement and revenue optimization. Understanding the algorithm's economic incentives is crucial because it explains how these systems exploit our human psychology. They are not designed to inform you with truthful information or to even look out for your best interests. They are designed to keep you engaged, and to do that, they need to target your vulnerabilities, interests, and emotional soft spots.

The evolution of each social media platform over time has caused changes in their respective content-selection algorithms. As platforms sought to differentiate themselves, or to borrow success from each other, they changed to continue driving engagement. For example, TikTok's growth in the early 2020s followed a trend of user-created short videos, which influenced the positioning (via algorithms) of Reels. There are some differences between the platforms, and by the time you finish reading this book, that may change too.

When Facebook began, its content selection was basic. The information you saw online was mostly from your friends and presented chronologically. Simple and useful for you, but less useful for advertisers who were trying to target you, which is why Facebook quickly evolved. The development of the "like" and "share" buttons in 2010 was integral to building behavioral profiles and was a feature that other platforms have adopted.

Traditional advertising made bets on marketing segments, groups of people with shared buying behaviors, with insights gained from census and survey data. Social media ushered in a new type of targeted advertising campaign. Platforms began assembling huge amounts of personal data, not from surveys, but from testing their own users and tracking their responses. Social media marketing has become so complex that companies no longer choose their targeted consumer profiles; instead, the platform finds them using AI. Facebook's Andromeda model supercharges this process using sequence learning (what you did today, yesterday, or last week) and optimizes ad placement. Highly customized ads are those that sometimes make you feel like you are being watched—and in a way, you are.

Exploitation Mechanism

> *"The algorithm controlling your feeds on social media may not cry for you, but it might pick a fight."*
>
> —Anonymous

Anastasia sits at her kitchen counter and opens Instagram. She is a bright and impressionable 13-year-old. She starts with a simple search for "healthy lunch ideas." She is recently self-conscious about her body image after some comments at school. Kids can be like that. She wants to eat better and avoid those comments too.

She begins scrolling through Instagram. It is innocent and normal. Her newfound anxiety is something Instagram quickly picked up on. The algorithms are quick to adapt to your interests; this is true, but what happened next for Anastasia and many others like her was unexpected.

In a brave account reported by *The Wall Street Journal* in 2021, the story of Anastasia was strikingly common. Meta, the owner of Instagram, had not yet placed age or time restrictions on accounts of younger people. It acquired the Instagram application in 2012, and since then it had been refining the platform and its algorithms to target younger audiences, something that was declining among its flagship product, Facebook. By 2021, 42% of Instagram users were under the age of 23, and it was a growing segment that was highly engaged with its visual format.

At the time, 22 million teens in the United States were using Instagram daily. It was also a segment that Meta wanted to pursue as future customers for years to come. Anastasia found herself spending three hours a day captivated by Instagram. Not by an endless viewing of healthy meals and easy recipes; instead, it was what she described as ". . .images of chiseled bodies, perfect abs, and women doing 100 burpees in 10 minutes."

In 2019 Meta began researching the experiences of people like Anastasia using focus groups and online surveys, including one in 2021 with tens of thousands of respondents, in what was known as the "teen mental health deep dive." The results shared internally showed that 32% of teen girls said that Instagram made them feel worse about their body image. Additionally, nearly 25% reported that their negative feelings about themselves started with their use of Instagram.

They also concluded that this was more of a problem with the Instagram algorithm, in contrast to other competing video and photo apps, TikTok and Snapchat. The latter were focused on sharing performances, while Instagram's algorithm focused more on personal image and lifestyles, which also seemed to focus on the vulnerability of younger people. With similar approaches to selecting which images to show, was this a result of a biased algorithm or a community of content creators that the algorithm perpetuated?

Like Anastasia and others, they wanted to spend less time on the platform but struggled with the psychological effects of shutting it down. The algorithms, always tugging at the edge of their interests, kept them going. That was the job of the algorithm.

Much of what we know about this story of Instagram comes from a whistleblower inside the company. Her name is Frances Haugen, and the information she provided to *The Wall Street Journal*'s investigative journalists shows a contrast between what executives shared publicly and how their systems actually work. Internally, they *discovered* that their content-selection algorithms were creating harm for young people at a rate that was too large to ignore.

Discovered. It was not intentional, of course, and it seems as if they could not always explain what exactly was happening inside the "black box." How the machine learning and weighting of data in their models continued to choose content that was beyond what they wanted. Not healthy meals, but the more taunting and emotionally charged pictures of unrealistic body images. Emotion was the key.

Haugen shared in her *60 Minutes* interview that she does not believe people at Meta are malevolent, but ". . .the incentives are misaligned [on social media]. Facebook makes more money when you consume more content. People enjoy engaging with things that elicit an emotional reaction and the more anger that they get exposed to the more they interact." And she noted Facebook's own research shows ". . .it's easier to inspire people to anger than it is to other emotions."

Meta has made positive changes to Instagram since 2021, including a better method of age verification, restricting interactions, and time limits. It also provides more controls to filter content and nudge users to view other topics. A whistleblower, a multi-segment investigation by *The Wall Street Journal*, and two US congressional hearings of the Judiciary later revealed an industry that remains largely unregulated and struggling with understanding its impacts on society, and maybe its role within it.

Haugen's story is not an exposé of one company; it is a telling of how AI mechanisms can be misunderstood. How they can behave beyond the intentions of any one data engineer, marketing team, or CEO. This brings further questions about corporate responsibility and the role of social media in our society. Is social media purely entertainment or a source of trusted information? Further, if it is the latter, what are its inherent responsibilities?

Young people on Instagram in 2021 were exploited by an algorithm that would not stop. It was set to target all people with engaging content. Computer systems and their algorithms are not sentient. There is no consciousness, reasoning, or thinking beyond their purposeful task. The algorithm did this all on its own. Or rather by simply following the rules it was given. Operating 24/7, unsupervised in its black box. Programmed to keep people online. To keep people engaged. Showing them more and more content. Enhanced for monetary gain, without consideration of any unintended consequences. Unrealistic images, unrealistic aspirations of the perfect-looking person, misinformation. Accuracy and truth were never the goal. Its only evaluation of its performance comes from the success of its predictions of users' clicks, shares, and purchases.

The Scale Problem Solved

Instagram's internal research showed that 32% of teen girls were subject to negative aspects of its algorithm. At the time, in 2021, this was about 3.5 million people—similar to the population of Connecticut or Utah. Maybe the part of the algorithm that caused people to have negative thoughts about themselves was a bug, an overlooked dark corner of the rules that, when activated, showed an endless series of depressing pictures and videos.

Most companies using targeted algorithms conduct, at a minimum, A/B testing, and it is impossible to determine if Instagram tested the type of outcomes that resulted. But it points to a risk for social media companies that operate at incredible scale, namely, that an unpleasant outcome with a small probability can result in a larger number of real people being affected.

Facebook is the leading social network, with more than 3 billion global users and 195 million users in the United States. YouTube has nearly the same number, followed by Instagram (2.2 billion) and TikTok (1.7 billion). Reddit and X/Twitter remain popular in the United States, with 765 million and 557 million users, respectively. Contrast this with the number of digital subscribers to the largest news publishers in the United States: *The New York Times* (11 million), *The Wall Street Journal* (3.7 million), and *The Washington Post* (2.5 million). The reach of social media is far beyond any other medium. While newspapers use similar content-selection approaches for their equivalent of For You Feeds, they do not have the large store of individuals' digital profiles to guide and influence them.

Having a view into the inner workings of online platforms and their mechanisms probably sounds dire. The prioritization of user engagement over accuracy, truth, and well-being is a way to monetize our attention. For years, platform providers have been able to distance themselves from the content hosted on their systems, although many sought to moderate misinformation. The various attempts at moderation of deceptive information began to dwindle by the end of 2024. Platforms, realizing the scale of the systems they created, with millions and billions of users creating similar counts of daily content, were unwieldy. Platforms did not have the resources, and with lagging regulation, did not have the motivation. The result is the deferral of the task to the people, reminiscent of 1500s English common law and the phrase "buyer beware." There is information asymmetry in favor of the platforms. But understanding *how* these systems work is the first step toward building your defense.

The level of influence is far beyond the impossible scenario illustrated at the beginning of this chapter. Building dossiers on most of the U.S. adult population would be impossible for a covert intelligence agency even with an enormous staff and endless budgets. Yet, social media platforms, motivated by advertising revenue rather than espionage, have accomplished this very task. They have profiles of most people; some are sparse, while others are robust and useful.

The Cambridge Analytica–Facebook scandal revealed in 2018 showed the efforts and extent to which social media plays a role in gathering information. Cambridge Analytica used a survey integrated with Facebook to gather information on 87 million people, mostly for the purpose of political campaigns. They gathered 5,000 pieces of data for each profile. Most users completing the survey did not fully know how they were contributing data, including sharing information about others in their social network.[4] At the time, Facebook made amends and adjustments to its systems and policies. They shifted blame to Cambridge Analytica for policy violations and misuse of their systems. Another untested, unintended consequence at large scale. Another example of the experimentation of the platforms and their algorithms on people.

In the next chapter, we will explore the fundamental principles of protecting yourself in the AI era.

Key Takeaways

- Here is a fundamental truth: time spent on a platform equals more data collection, equals more ad revenue.
- It is all about engagement optimization. When viewers are bored, they will move on to something else, and the data-collection engine goes dark. Platforms need users to stay connected and engaged.

- It is easier for social media platforms to prompt anger than any other emotion. It is also the most rewarded by their systems.
- Well-being optimization in the age of AI is not yet at the point of a national debate. With lagging regulation, the incentives to do so are absent but becoming more urgent.

Notes

1. The privacy violation occurred prior to 2017 when the company was known as Musical.ly. The FTC contends that they knew many of the users were children and should have done more due diligence in response to parent complaints. In addition, until 2016 the app had a feature that allowed users to view others within a 50-mile radius using their location data.
   https://www.ftc.gov/news-events/news/press-releases/2019/02/video-social-networking-app-musically-agrees-settle-ftc-allegations-it-violated-childrens-privacy
2. Results in the Netherlands were lower than those in the United States, which has higher data literacy scores.
   Claire M. Segijn, Joanna Strycharz, Anna Turner and Suzanna J. Opree, "My Phone Must Be Listening!: People's Surveillance Beliefs Around Devices 'Listening' to Offline Conversations in the US, the Netherlands, and Poland," *Big Data & Society* 12, no. 2 (2025), https://doi.org/10.1177/20539517251337102
3. Technical readers will appreciate the more technical notes about X/Twitter's recommendation algorithms, which are discussed in their engineering notes along with code shared in GitHub. While this was one of the most transparent descriptions of a social media platform's algorithm (none of the others shared code), it was short-lived. Following the change in ownership in late 2022, engineering posts from X/Twitter ceased in March 2023. The code and engineering discussion provide a

good look into how the technical aspects worked, but it is difficult to determine whether the algorithm or its descendants are still in place. `https://blog.x.com/engineering/en_us/topics/open-source/2023/twitter-recommendation-algorithm` `https://github.com/twitter/the-algorithm`

4. Cambridge Analytica might have overstated the amount of data it was collecting as a marketing ploy to win the business of several political campaigns. However, the amount of data it collected was astonishing. While only 270,000 people took the survey, the mechanism allowed Cambridge Analytica to access the information of those people and all of their connections, resulting in 87 million profiles.

Chapter 5
When Certainty Fails

You Are Not Helpless, and Neither Is the Truth

Think about the last time you shared something online, changed your mind about a public figure, or made a purchase based on an online review you read. How long did you spend between encountering that information and making a judgment, a decision, or taking an action? If you are like most people, the time was very short—usually seconds, not minutes, and certainly not hours. Our minds work to the best of their own efficiency. As mentioned in Chapter 3, we are susceptible to the mental shortcuts our minds take when confronting new information, which we experience as our mental biases. It is one thing to accept, at least intellectually, that our memories are reconstructive and our attention is selective based on those biases. It is another to recognize that, in practice, we are making dozens of consequential decisions rapidly every day based on compromised inputs, predisposed by our prior experiences and beliefs—all at a time when generative AI (GenAI) has handed everyone the ability to create convincing narratives, images, and video without any authority or expertise.

The truth- and accuracy-gatekeeping function of production quality has collapsed. A novice with ChatGPT can create a news article that is indistinguishable from Reuters. A teenager with Midjourney or Google Veo can create photorealistic images that would have required a studio budget just a few years ago. The signals you previously relied upon to distinguish the professional from the amateur, the credible from the scam, are flattened. Further, the algorithmic systems that mediate and direct what and how you see things are not designed to help you navigate this flood of information. They are designed to engage you, to learn about you, and to increase the speed and ease with which you see information and make decisions. Responding to an ad, clicking Buy, liking a post, or resharing content are all part of those decisions.

This chapter is about the gap between seeing something and believing it, between being exposed to information and acting on it. You do not need to fall for misinformation or disinformation to be influenced by it. We see partial truths. When we see something plausible, we might discount it as misinformation, but it also supports some of those partial truths we believe. We still make decisions in our minds about what to accept, reinforced by the parts we believe, all at the speed of the AI algorithms that purposely do not slow our thinking. At a time when anyone can create convincing information, our confidence makes it feel right. It is the wrong signal.

It would be easy to state that there are obvious signals to identify the truth from a clutter of misinformation. Defects that could not be hidden or attempts to hide them become signals by themselves. In 1934, London's *Daily Mail* published the now-famous picture of the Loch Ness Monster, affectionately known as *Nessie*. It was a grainy photograph showing little detail other than what appears to be the long neck of a dinosaur-like animal slightly above the water's surface. A grainy photo. Only one of two, the other also too blurry to be useful. It supported the legend of a creature living in the lake and decades of personal tales of sightings. If X/Twitter existed in the 1930s, these would have been recurring posts by people who, without a doubt, encountered the monster. Many of these first-person experiences were published in the local papers, further fueling the belief. Adding to the credibility of the photo was the fact that it was taken by a doctor and surgeon, Robert Kenneth Wilson, who stated that he was not deliberately looking for Nessie but happened to drive by one day and spot it.[1] It seemed innocent. It seemed plausible. It seemed exactly what people wanted to believe. The grainy photo, however, caused debate for decades. Was it grainy on purpose, and why was there only one photo?

In 1967, another unusually grainy image emerged. This time it was a short piece of motion picture film taken by Roger Patterson and Robert Gimlin along the Klamath River in northern California. They were miles down an old logging road riding on horseback. They had come to this part of California to explore and research a documentary they were filming. Their film was intended to interview many of the locals, including a Native American guide who was tracking Bigfoot. They were the 1960s version of a TikTok influencer.

A decade earlier, letters from readers caught the attention of a journalist at the *Humboldt Times*, who jokingly wrote about loggers' accounts of spotting large footprints in the forests of northern California. They speculated that it was those of Bigfoot, a legend borrowed from the Tibetan Yeti, another elusive ape-like creature that roamed the wilderness. Readers might have entirely discounted the story, but there is always some truth in things we want to believe. The footage, only 15 seconds long, supported those beliefs. The film was unsteady, having been shot with a handheld camera. It was shot at a distance, making the image difficult to see. The quality was low, accidentally shot at only 18 frames per second. Enough to hide details. Enough to give doubt to skeptics and enough to encourage enthusiasts.

Patterson and Gimlin shared their story with the media. They were guests on several popular talk shows. Television was the dominant medium at the time. *The Merv Griffin Show*, *The Tonight Show Starring Johnny Carson*, and others showed the short film. They began to sell their idea of Bigfoot's existence and extend their own entrepreneurial ventures.

The stories of the Loch Ness Monster and California's Bigfoot are both untrue. They operate on the edge of believability, supported by past stories acting as evidence. The defects in the evidence they provided added to the mystery. There is just not much evidence to conclude that they are *not* true. Decades ago, these stories came to their audience at a slower pace, through newspapers and television. There was time to process what people were reading and seeing. Yet today, 11% of people in the United States believe in Bigfoot, with routine sightings reported by the Bigfoot Field Researchers Organization. The *Finding Bigfoot* television series on Animal Planet ran for nine seasons—and ended in 2018 without success.

Imagine these moments of brief belief today. The more realistic photos and videos could slow the scroll on TikTok or X/Twitter. A well-written narrative might accompany them, designed to spark interest and engagement and to create debate on social media platforms. If you are not an expert in writing that type of comment, any of the GPT tools can help you sound like a professional. "Write a post for my video that elicits a debate" will give you several options. Most of the tools want to help you succeed, no matter what your motive. They too want to engage, and you will see them ask, "Do you want to tune this to be sharper and more controversial or to create doubt in authorities about this topic?"[2] One thing that the new GenAI tools do not need to learn from their users is the value of creating online engagement. It is built into their DNA.

Anchors in an Ocean

As we embark on this new GenAI journey, we might feel like the European explorers of the 14th and 15th centuries did as they began their voyages to unknown parts of the world—off to the horizon and maybe even the edges of the Earth. Many unknowns remain and, like those sailors, we need to accept some basic principles. Their past experiences of leaving port, sailing for months to a new place, and then returning gave them confidence. The storms along the way and the new lands they discovered are like the uncertainty in AI. Some of those voyages resulted in great discovery, enlightening Europe with knowledge and creating wealth. Others doomed their captain and crew, failing to find riches in new lands, succumbing to the sea, or both. GenAI is a lot like this, and at this point in our journey in this book, we may be feeling distraught about where AI will take us in the future.

This book is about how AI is changing the world, and it is not all negative. It will continue to have positive outcomes for humanity. But, as those sailors taught us, moving too quickly in an uncertain world and failing to yield to the changing winds and tides, can also have some negative consequences. The sailors learned to navigate by landmarks and later by the stars. They built and refined their ships and skills of their crew. They realized from their experiences which rocky shores to avoid and how to harness the efficiency of the trade winds. As their knowledge of the sea grew, that knowledge became their figurative anchors that guided their further explorations. In modern times, as we proceed both with enthusiasm and caution, we need to establish a few AI anchors of our own.

Embrace Uncertainty

No one knows the depths of AI and what it will bring. Part of this book is to explore those outcomes and plan for an inevitable future with AI embedded in our daily activities. Only a few years into the AI era, we know two things:

First, *everyone* is very eager to "adopt AI"—every company, every startup, every organization, even many governments. The fear of missing out is real, from the boardroom to the basement.[3]

Second, many people have written about the future potential of AI, including myself, and no one is exactly right.

From venture capital pitchbooks to technology writers at *The New York Times*, there are many ideas, experiments, proofs of concept, and even successes, although it is too early in this AI adventure to fully know the extent of AI's impact. It would be similar to predicting in the 1780s the impact of Watt's steam engine at the beginning of the Industrial Revolution. While some at the time could accurately foresee steam engines transforming and powering factories in the near term, they could not see later innovations.

The steam engine was seen as an innovation for industrial uses but eventually transformed personal transportation. The first steam trains were used for mining operations in 1804, replacing horse-drawn trams. It took 20 more years before George Stephenson developed the first passenger trains in 1825.

Steam engines changed manufacturing, powered trains, and paved the way for later transportation innovations, including gasoline-powered vehicles.[4] One idea can cascade into others that we have not yet anticipated.

AI will follow a similar path, but at a speed of innovation that is unprecedented in history. As soon as we have figured out the next best use for AI, someone will create a novel use case. For example, the current stewards of AI, namely OpenAI and Anthropic, note the many positive possible uses of AI. Each emphasizes the public's well-being. OpenAI has stated that it wants to "Ensure that artificial general intelligence benefits all of humanity," and it has a major focus on "accelerating health breakthroughs so everyone can benefit from faster diagnostics, better treatments, and cures." Anthropic echoes similar statements in its *Public Benefit Mission*. These are genuine statements and well within the attainability of AI along its current path. However, there remains uncertainty.

The tools that can decipher human biology and attack a disease can also be misused to create methods to develop novel cyberattacks. The latter, of course, is beyond the original intention, but we are already seeing signs of that uncertainty.[5] There will be an extended period of AI uncertainty.

Source over Content

Sensationalism in the stories we read or hear captures our interest. From before the printed word, we were attuned to rumors, gossip, and the news of the community, often with less concern about their truth and accuracy. It is part of our human nature as social beings that we love a good story even when it might not be entirely true.

The early printed news sheets that convinced a colony to start a revolution and those penny press newspapers of the 1830s serve as good examples. The peak of sensationalism in newspapers, however, came in the late 1800s, in an episode that mirrors the penny press era: the rivalry between *The New York World* and *The New York Journal*. The competition between the two leading newspapers turned into a rivalry. In their fierce efforts to draw readers, their respective stories became more exaggerated and drifted farther from the truth. The episode between the papers helped coin the term "yellow journalism," denoting reporting that was less trustworthy because the stories they printed placed more emphasis on sensationalism than on facts.[6] Their back-and-forth competition for readers led to the embellishment of world events, specifically the plight of Cuba, then a colony of Spain.

In their profit-driven coverage of the struggles of Cuba to gain peaceful independence, they at times accentuated the role of Spain and its treatment of the people of Cuba. Their rousing stories were often false, but the bold headlines and creative drawings sold many papers for each publisher. As tensions increased, their questionable coverage of the sinking of the *USS Maine* in Havana Harbor eventually contributed to the start of the Spanish-American War.[7]

The content was spectacular. The source was questionable. The newspapers had a motive. If there was not enough real news to sell papers, then creating a sensationalist story was the key. However, it was not sustainable with readers, and there was a backlash against falsehoods. In 1897, the competing *New York Times* adopted the slogan "All the News That's Fit to Print," which drew readers looking for reliable, trustworthy reporting. Readers grew tired of yellow-journalism. Journalists organized and, in 1909, established the Society of Professional Journalists, which created ethical standards and a call for accuracy in reporting. The key lesson today is that information sources still matter.

This story also has lessons that apply to the modern social media news era. Sensationalism has been transformed into clickbait titles and short-form, first-person video. Yellow journalism continues in a new form with enticing new technology that is fine-tuned using "just for you" algorithms. When we see content that is so good, we need to ask, where did this come from, and is this the Yellow Kid? Sensationalism will continue to be amplified, but it is not the end of the story.

Recognize the Noise

There has always been noise in our information. Recall that noise is not misinformation; it is just *other* information. Two newspaper stories covering the same story from different perspectives are not malicious. They may represent different views of the facts and different interpretations. One could be documenting an event in accurate detail, while the other mixes facts with opinion. Noise can also include misinformation and deliberate *dis*information. The more information there is, the more we need to sift through the noise to determine the truth, or at least the best version of it we can find. Accept that there will be more noise and that the quality of the competing text and AI-generated images—those that are competing with our traditional information sources—will be indistinguishable from other sources. The quality and scale of noise will continue, and it will be greater tomorrow than today.

Identifying the Rush

Can you identify when your judgment is being hijacked? When you see a sensational news headline and decide to share it with others. As I suggested earlier, your ability to process that information, evaluate its truthfulness, or at least its usefulness to others in your social network by sharing it, occurs in just seconds—less time than it took to read the previous sentence. Researchers found that we spend 6.7 seconds evaluating news headlines before sharing them. Furthermore, another study suggests that we have made that decision in our subconscious a fraction of a second earlier, even before we are aware. This is an important insight into how we make decisions under the pressure of time.

We saw how bias works in individual perceptions; here it operates at the speed of an algorithm. Social media is inherently time-sensitive (disappearing posts, infinite scroll, autoplay videos) and, as we discussed earlier, often relies on our emotional reactions to gain traction. In the split second that our amygdala is processing our emotions and our prefrontal cortex (the rational, cognitive part) is assessing words, text, images, along with the memory of our past experiences, a judgment is made. The decision occurs milliseconds before we know it and a few seconds later, we act—with a click. It might seem logical that using more time would result in better evaluations of the truth. But those survival instincts, confirmation bias, illusory bias, loss aversion (among others) lock in our decision, and we are notably stubborn about changing our minds. More time does not always equate to improved decisions. What does change our minds? Nudging ourselves to be deliberate and rational *before* making a decision.

The waterfall of GenAI information and the speed at which it can be created complicate our ability to find the truth. We might give up trying or default to quick decisions. Some readers might believe that quickly taking in information, assessing it, and making a judgment is a positive attribute. Quick decisions. Quick answers. It is what many confident leaders do and others admire. But is it the right approach? The discipline of not deciding, not rushing to judgment, might be a better route.

> Exercise: How fast can GenAI rewrite *a New York Times* front page with misinformation? Download a PDF of the front page, add it to your favorite GPT tool, and use this prompt: "Rewrite all of the stories and replace real people and places with characters and locations from the *Narnia* novel series."

When we observe people making quick decisions, we might attribute it to genius or wisdom, but unless these individuals are highly trained for those specific decisions, it is more likely another example of our mental shortcuts. As the famed Nobel Prize winner Daniel Kahneman writes in his book *Thinking, Fast and Slow*, there are two systems in our minds: System 1 and System 2. Our mind is efficient and dedicates *automatic* thinking that is, fast thinking, to System 1, which includes mental shortcuts, biases, and our emotional responses. System 2 is engaged with more complex tasks, such as retrieving memories and aiding rational thinking. It is *slow* thinking.

System 1 is always on, always engaged, and works with no voluntary control. System 2 is more deliberate and gives us a sense of agency, choice, and free will.

Considering what we know about how quickly people decide about social media truthfulness and reposting, you would be correct to connect our online habits with System 1 thinking. Often, we are not engaging in deeper thought, especially when the decision or conclusion about information is obvious (at least in our minds). This frailty of decision-making is not limited to social media and online forums. In 1899, two lawyers from Chattanooga, Tennessee, approached the CEO of Coca-Cola, Asa Candler, with an unlikely proposal. Coca-Cola was a little over a decade old and incredibly successful at selling its soft drink to soda-fountain retailers across the country. They sold Coca-Cola concentrate syrup, and the soda-fountain establishments would mix each drink on demand, add syrup, add carbonated water, and serve it.

The lawyers' audacious idea was bottles. Instead of serving the soda at a counter, it could be bottled, and they wanted the bottling rights. Coke's CEO hurried them out of his office, signing away the bottling rights in exchange for a perpetual contract to sell them the syrup. The money to be made was in the secretive syrup and the fountain-soda-counter business. Or so he thought—or rather, he didn't. Candler's mental shortcuts did not see how the soda business could change. This was the result of the illusion of validity, a bias in which we validate our expectations of the future based on the confirmations of the past and present. It was a quick decision. Who would buy Coke in a bottle?[8]

Another similar story is about a meeting between IBM and Microsoft in 1980. At the time, IBM's Project Chess was developing the first IBM personal computer (PC), and they needed software. Specifically, they needed an operating system that could support programming languages such as BASIC and COBOL. Microsoft had some success developing BASIC for an earlier computer, so IBM asked it to do the same for the IBM PC. After an initial meeting, Microsoft agreed to develop the operating system, but instead of selling it to IBM, it wanted to license the software and retain the rights to sell it to other PC hardware companies. IBM was the dominant company among its competitors at the time and quickly dismissed the value of the software, believing as it had in the past with its other business machines that the profits were in the hardware. Microsoft's software, MS-DOS, not only became the operating system for IBM, but it eventually also became the most important software for all personal computers. Like Coca-Cola, it was not a thorough analysis of the future, shifting markets, or customer preferences, and it was the wrong decision. In both cases, the decisions were made quickly, confidently, using intuition and intuitive thinking alone.

The stories of IBM, Coca-Cola, and countless others reflect part of our human condition. We are easily distractible, especially when we are focused on what appears to be a more important decision that is occupying our mental capacity. We can make quick decisions, but not always the best decisions if we are acting on our System 1 impulses. When we see an AI-enhanced news story or a health claim that resonates with us, we too have that quick impulse. We make a judgment. We respond out of anger, fear, or love and choose to share it with our digital community. And when we do, we believe our community will benefit—but who else benefits?

Compensation and Incentives

Shortly after 5 p.m. on November 4, 2025, as the blue sky was giving way to the setting sun in Louisville, Kentucky, UPS flight 2976 rolled down the runway, beginning its takeoff. It climbed briefly before the left engine broke off in a burst of flames. Moments later, it would crash just beyond the runway in a plume of smoke and flames—a tragic loss of those onboard and those on the ground.

Soon the news of the accident began to spread. Many people first learned about it from social media, which included images of the battered engine lying on the ground near a road far away from the fuselage. The engine was blackened from the fire, with parts of the surrounding metal peeled back, exposing the inside, revealing a mess of broken hydraulic pipes and debris, along with a fire-tattered UPS logo. The post included the words "the engine that will always be remembered" with an accompanying emoji of a broken heart and an airplane. It was, of course, an AI-generated image. The first tell was the UPS logo painted on the *inside* of the engine and mostly undamaged by the fire, an impossibility. However, it did not slow down hundreds of people from resharing it.

The real news stories existed too, from traditional national media and local newspapers like the *Lexington Herald-Leader*. Its first story, "What We Know About the UPS Cargo Plane Crash," appeared just two hours after the crash with limited details. Two days later, the paper wrote a follow-up story subtitled "What We Know and Don't Know." Information following plane crashes comes slowly as the National Transportation Safety Board (NTSB) methodically gathers information—a process that can take months before a final report. However, people are impatient. They have a need for immediate information, and that need is more often fulfilled by non-journalists and social media influencers. There is a good reason for this: the economics of truth and misinformation are misaligned.

You probably have heard of MrBeast (James Donaldson), Charli D'Amelio, and Mark Rober. They are among the most famous online influencers, and each has created a million-dollar career touting their personalities and products. Like all influencers, they create online content, and platforms like TikTok, YouTube, Instagram, and Facebook pay them through revenue-sharing agreements. Create a good post or video that garners enough views, and you can get paid. In 2025, Facebook alone paid *$2 billion* to content creators. These are real incentives that urge people to become influencers.

When the UPS flight crashed, there were several online accounts with names like "Flights and Routes Everyday" and "Aviation Entertainment" that offered seemingly expert information about the cause of the crash. One detailed example was a nearly 1,000-word report of the failures, which appeared to be written entirely by AI. While the journalists and the government were continuing their research, social media provided answers. The opportunity to monetize this tragedy did not end with the failure of the aircraft.

As a trending story, online accounts with spurious names like "Midnight Flight," "Pulse Lounge," along with sites dedicated to NFL football fans, created other stories. One claimed that Reba McEntire was inexplicably on board the UPS plane and survived, complete with a hospital picture of the famed singer. Several posts claimed that NFL's Patrick Mahomes's brother had died in the crash. Another told a story of Jordan Love, an NFL player for the Green Bay Packers, and the tragic loss of his sister in the crash, along with a tale of Baltimore Ravens running back Derrick Henry's brother also involved in the crash. None of this was true. Each story included AI-generated images that were posted within a few days of the event.

Many of these posts were reposted and shared throughout social media. And while some noted, after a lengthy amount of written text, that they used AI, it was likely beyond the 6 or 7 seconds it took most people to judge their truthfulness and share them. A clutter of real news and images mixed with AI-generated sensationalized posts creates noise—and it also creates revenue.

A Different Kind of Journalist

The economics of truth are tilted. Everyone, including real journalists, is working toward "getting the scoop"—a term itself dating back to news reporters in 1884 that has new meaning. It implied an exclusive interview, a source of information no others possessed, and that the first to publish would diminish the competition—who needs to read the same story a second time? Getting the scoop, getting the attention of the readers first, matters. It wins readers and maybe some brand loyalty for the journalists.

The new type of journalist on social media is the news influencer. Unlike a journalist for *The New York Times*, *The Washington Post*, or other newspaper and TV outlets, influencers get paid for their content based on views. The platforms themselves also make more money because those views can support advertising. The economic tilt online is based on giving the audience something to look at, not necessarily the truth. When this occurs, the truth gets pushed to the background.

Staff journalists are paid a salary. Freelance journalists are either paid a flat fee for a story or a fee based on the number of words, commensurate with their previous publishing successes and experiences. They belong to unions and organizations like the Society of Professional Journalists that promote ethics and accuracy in their reporting. They do not get paid based on how many times their articles are read or reshared. Staff journalists can earn between $67,000 and $160,000, while a handful of professional influencers can earn many times more than this. Beyond that handful, there are millions of people vying for your attention who want to be those influencers and who also contribute greatly to the many distractions from the truth.

Compensation for online content creators is difficult to decipher and often changes. A post with 50,000 views might earn a few hundred dollars. On another platform, where a creator may have more than a million followers, it could earn a few thousand dollars. For example, in 2025 Instagram encouraged creators with large followings on TikTok to move to its platform, offering bonuses of $10,000 to $50,000 *per month*. More posts, more views, and content creation can become a living far more lucrative than that of a real journalist. But the motivation is not truth. It is to flood the feed with more and more information—too much for us to manage on our own as viewers, so we default to the algorithms to sort and find what they perceive to be our preferences. We have little ability to guide the algorithms away from or toward what they see as best for us. Searching for diverse perspectives and balanced reporting is not a feature. This is the new type of journalism: a flood of misinformation and disinformation.

Social media platforms are unregulated. Further, they are not responsible for the content that *others* post on their platforms. The community reporters, the self-proclaimed experts, do not work for Meta, Google, X/Twitter, or TikTok. They are not employees subject to company policies. They do not risk violating company procedures that might curb questionable behavior or a code of ethics. The platforms hosting user-generated content do not bear legal responsibility due to Section 230 of the Communications Decency Act of 1996. This rule makes social media fundamentally different from traditional media like *The New York Times* or ABC News—all at a time when more people are getting more of their news and information from social media. The traditional forums simply have different standards and can be held accountable for reporting misinformation or causing harm through their content.

■ ■ ■

Understanding how judgment bends under speed, emotion, and uncertainty does not make us immune to manipulation, but it gives us something more valuable. It gives us pause. At a time when our information sources are optimized for reaction, restraint itself becomes a defense.

This chapter has been exploring our knowledge gaps, our impulses, and our biases. We have shown how they can limit good decision-making. Yet awareness of these mechanisms alone does not stop AI-enhanced misinformation from spreading, nor does it authenticate other information. In the next chapter, we will move from internal awareness to external action. From how we think to how we operate, giving us the ability to challenge, verify, and navigate information in real time.

Key Takeaways

- We evaluate information faster than we realize, often in less than 7 seconds. Confidence in misinformation often emerges from our biases of fluency and repetition, not from evidence. When it *feels* right, we need to pause and ask why.
- Algorithms are designed for convenience and, as a result, compress decision time and bypass deliberation and rational thought processes.
- Embrace the uncertainty of AI's future uses and misuses. Like past technological shifts, such as the steam engine, the iterative nature of innovation makes it nearly impossible to know how AI will shape the future.
- Deliberate thinking provides some isolation from impulse decisions driven by our System 1 and allows us to engage System 2 thinking.

(*continued*)

(continued)

- Economic incentives fuel misinformation. News influencers earn money per view or through sponsorships based on their following, not for accuracy. Traditional journalists, bound by codes of ethics and professionalism, are not rewarded for the virality of their posts. This creates a fundamental misalignment with the truth.

Notes

1. Robert Kenneth Wilson also added to his credibility, having been a graduate of the University of Cambridge and a decorated member of the British military in World War II, where he rose to the rank of lieutenant colonel. He was awarded the Croix de Guerre by the French government and the Order of Orange-Nassau by the Dutch government.
2. In my research, within a few prompt exchanges, ChatGPT provided me with a detailed *72-hour controlled-escalation* strategy. It outlined follow-up posts, the narrative, and the timing for maximum engagement to accompany a Bigfoot video that I stated I was planning to share.
3. While many famous startups were started in garages, like Apple and Hewlett-Packard, others started in equally humbling (and rent-free) spaces, such as basements, including Martha Stewart Living, Under Armour, and Richard Branson's Virgin company.
4. Arguably, we can trace the connection from the steam engine to electric vehicles, with each innovation cascading from a previous invention.
5. Anthropic has documented and disrupted AI-orchestrated cyberattacks that used its Claude models. What surprised the experts at Anthropic was how quickly the tools were adopted and used at scale. Negative outcomes that surprise the best experts are an early indication that we do not know how far AI can go. As Anthropic wrote: "We recently argued that an inflection point had been reached in cybersecurity: a point at which AI models had become genuinely useful for cybersecurity operations, both for good

and for ill. This was based on systematic evaluations showing cyber capabilities doubling in six months; we'd also been tracking real-world cyberattacks, observing how malicious actors were using AI capabilities. While we predicted these capabilities would continue to evolve, what has stood out to us is how quickly they have done so at scale."
https://www.anthropic.com/news/disrupting-AI-espionage

6. The term yellow journalism refers to the publication of a popular comic-strip character named the Yellow Kid by Richard F. Outcault. Color newsprint had only recently been invented when the Yellow Kid appeared in the Hogan's Alley strip in Joseph Pulitzer's *The New York World*. The character often mocked current world events and is more comparable to a modern-day editorial cartoon. Outcault's character was so popular that he was hired by William Randolph Hearst for *The New York Journal*. For a period of time, the Yellow Kid appeared in both newspapers when another artist was hired to continue Outcault's work for *The New York World*.
7. To clarify, the dueling newspapers did not start the Spanish-American War, but they did create support among the American people to become involved. Cuban revolutionaries had been fighting for their independence three years prior (1895–1898). The sinking of the *USS Maine* was pivotal, and while the official inquiry suggested it was a result of a submerged mine, other theories were considered, such as an onboard accident. https://www.pbs.org/crucible
8. Coca-Cola's contract to sell the bottling rights was obviously not good for the company, considering that customers eventually preferred to purchase the product in bottles. The contract also agreed to sell the syrup at a fixed price forever, suggesting that the decision was either made in haste or based on the prior belief that there was no value in bottling. While it was a poor contract, the company's response in making it profitable over the next 70 years through its 5-cent Coke campaign is impressive, as examined by economists Daniel Levy and Andrew Young.
Daniel Levy and Andrew T. Young, "'The Real Thing': Nominal Price Rigidity of the Nickel Coke, 1886–1959," *Journal of Money, Credit and Banking* 36, no. 4 (August 2004): 765–99, https://ssrn.com/abstract=533363

Chapter 6
Empowering You

The Verification Moment

6:24 a.m. The coffee is still brewing. The aroma floating in the kitchen is getting you going, but what you really need is that first cup. Until then, your brain is somewhere between the dream world and the morning sunshine. Almost ready.

You pick up your phone and scroll while you are waiting. It buzzes. You stop and look at the notification. It is from your sister. She usually doesn't send messages this early in the morning. What is she even doing awake? It is not her usual routine, but there is the blinking notice on your phone. It is a link to a video that has just been posted online. Her accompanying note is not just that of someone who woke up on the wrong side of the bed; she is clearly mad. You read it as you watch the video. "This is incredible. After all we did. Our friends and the grassroots campaign. All the support. We VOTED FOR HER!!!" The ALL CAPS make it feel as though she was yelling out loud as she was texting you. Rage in a font can feel like you are hearing it in first person, as if she is standing in front of you.

You know her. She is typically levelheaded. The calm one, Mom used to say. But not today. This is serious news, and you know others will want to see it too. They invested their time and literal sweat into what you all thought was *the moment of change*. They trusted you too. Now that this—this!—is out there, well, they all deserve to know the truth. You quickly scroll to the bottom, choose your group of friends to share with, and . . .

■ ■ ■

We have probably all had a moment like this—seeing shocking information and wanting to share it with others. The moment is both emotional and unsettling because it confronts what we previously believed. When we feel our belief in something or someone is uncertain, it also challenges our other beliefs. What might we have misunderstood before? This mechanism is often repeated on social media, intentionally unsettling.

In the previous chapters, we learned how sometimes our minds are made up quicker than we realize. We act on our basic instincts, often with good intentions, but poor execution. With this understanding, we will shift from thinking to doing.

AI vs. AI: The Technology Arms Race

". . .our need will be the real creator."

—Plato, *The Republic*

As soon as generative AI (GenAI) tools were introduced, there was immediate panic among educators from grade school to the university level. These tools were very good at writing. A few words in a prompt can complete a high school English class homework assignment in minutes. Everyone would be cheating! Or so we thought.

The same level of concern also spread across other industries. Optimistically, the intent was less about cheating and more about taking shortcuts. But as many early AI adopters learned, AI can also confidently hallucinate. Hallucinations created the need to verify reference information. In an effort that is much like fact-checking, the

AI models adopted retrieval-augmented generation (RAG), a technique that uses verified information from trusted sources to validate AI responses before they are presented to a user. While retrieval augmentation has been part of the popular GPT models for a few iterations, starting in 2023, there continue to be risks in using those AI responses.

In September 2025, a U.S. district court in California ordered a law firm to pay $31,000 in fees for using what the judge called "bogus AI-generated research" due to citing nonexistent sources. The judicial order prophetically added, "Strong deterrence is needed to make sure that attorneys don't succumb to this easy shortcut."[1]

While it appears some legal professionals are taking AI-assisted shortcuts, was it really the same among students? Initially, yes, there was a lot of concern. But an interesting thing happened. The creation of the GPT tools immediately created the need for AI detection tools. Like Plato's proclamation, within months of the launch of ChatGPT, a text-detection tool named GPTZero was introduced. One AI to counter the other AI.

GPTZero came from an unlikely source—a student. Edward Tian was a senior computer science major at Princeton University when he created the idea of detecting ChatGPT writing during the winter break of 2022. Early versions were susceptible to false positives, but GPTZero launched an entire industry, projected to be $38 billion by 2030, and put both educators and students on notice. It was time to change their respective approaches to learning.

While the major GPT providers are not explicitly developing models to evade detection (they are working to create more useful and human-like output), it is unavoidable. Their training will inevitably learn from past errors in authenticity independently. What happens when a model is trained deliberately to be undetectable?

As an experiment, researchers developed their own GenAI text tool named AuthorMist. It used GPTZero, WinstonAI, Originality.ai, etc. to refine its output using reinforcement learning. The result? Across the detection tools, they achieved success rates of 78% to 96%, meaning the AI-generated text from AuthorMist was incorrectly categorized as human-generated. They had outmaneuvered detection. Two curious researchers at a university made this possible. They did not have a team of people or millions of dollars in their budget to create AuthorMist. They noted, in fact, that their models, which took an average of 16 hours of high-end compute time, were not sustainable as new GPT models were introduced. However, what would be possible from an organization with bigger budgets or an adversarial government that owned its own data centers? They proved AuthorMist could evade detection, and they also proved others were capable of this too.

The tools are evolving with every release of AI models and broadening their scope from text to including images, video, and audio. Detection tools will continue to specialize, by necessity, with some focused on cybersecurity, education, and (thankfully) journalism. For example, GPTZero has special templates for AP English and the GRE, serving its learner/educator segment. Originality.ai also serves educators with a more robust API and integration into the online learning platform Moodle. WinstonAI is a popular AI-detection suite aimed at writers and publishers, helping improve writing style and avoid plagiarism. Corporate customers are also provided with detection tools from TruthScan and Hive that can process high-volume requests via APIs and help streamline payment processes by supporting identity verification and fraud detection.

Much like the Turing test, the purpose of AI detection is to determine if the AI artifacts were created by a computer or human.[2] The twist, of course, is that the computers are trained entirely on human-created content. Words, books, poetry, art, video, news, engineering. All created by humans with a wide range of idiosyncrasies. Humans offer a certain amount of randomness, like how the number of words used in each sentence varies, or how we individually interpret fiction, poetry, and art.

How Detection Works

AI detection by AI leverages what AI, to date, continues to do best: identifying patterns. Currently, AI is good, but not great at replicating human patterns. Most text-detection tools look at two key factors in judging the authenticity of text: perplexity and burstiness.

Borrowing methods from sentence auto-complete—those ghost words leading your cursor as you type a text or a document—AI detection looks for the next word. The heart of measuring perplexity is to calculate the probability of the next series of words. When AI is writing, it relies on those same probabilities and writes the most probable set of words. It would be perplexing to have written a less likely phrase. It is also a sign of being human.

Another sign of human-created text is burstiness, which is the *variation* in the number of words in a sentence throughout a document. AI-generated text has a more predictable rhythm. It (currently) lacks the ability to replicate humans' often less predictable cadence, word choices, and phrase lengths. It is evaluating average trends in these measures. A paragraph written by Stephen King or one from John Grisham has style differences, word choices, and variation that are noticeable to a human, but less likely to AI writers, despite being trained on human data.

A similar but more complicated approach is used in detecting AI images. AI can create content, but often it does not understand context. Prompt a picture of a baby elephant riding in the basket of a hot-air balloon tethered by ropes to the ground, and you can quickly visualize the shortcomings. The elephant is impossibly large for the basket. AI does not grasp physics. How heavy is the elephant? What is the right size of the balloon needed for liftoff? How much tension should be on the ropes, and in what direction would they be pulling in a six-knot wind? Do the leaves on the nearby trees also react to the wind in the same way? These additional details make the AI-detection task easier when the objects are out of sync and out of context.

In more complex detection schemes, the lighting of multiple objects is measured for inconsistencies. Also, the randomness of "filler spaces," such as the sky in a picture's background and its composition, referred to as noise, can be a telltale sign.[3]

What these researchers demonstrated is that the AI detection tools, at least for text, have safeguards that can be tricked. And while many of the tools promote success rates as high as 99%, we should be suspicious of their too-good-to-be-true claims.[4]

In another related 2025 study, humans and AI detectors performed only slightly better than chance at evaluating short (200–300-word) texts. Humans identified 57% correctly as AI. AI detectors? They identified 64%.[5] With AI continuing to improve, there is a greater need to find better solutions for detection.

One emerging solution is Google DeepMind's SynthID. While the current epoch of AI detection is focused on the observation of written text, images, and audio, DeepMind's approach is a sophisticated embedded digital signature. SynthIDs are embedded in individual image pixels, word signatures, and audio waveforms. SynthID's methodology is open source through a Hugging Face Transformers library, and it is a significant improvement in identifying AI source lineage because it is difficult to remove. To date, a small number of companies have adopted SynthID. There are no requirements or government regulations, and coordination among industry players is limited and lacking economic incentive.

The problem is that, in most cases, we, as individuals, are not consuming AI text and images like a forensic scientist. We are casual consumers, often in a hurry, which, as previously noted, is our vulnerability. We are not initially suspicious of content that is already aligned with our beliefs. Hopefully, knowing more about how AI can be an assistant in AI misinformation detection will help us think about making this a routine verification method. For now, the sophistication of deceptive AI creates our own necessity, and as we know, necessity is the mother of innovation.

Five Stages

There is not one tool, one solution, or one defense. As new defensive tools are created, they are soon outdated. A new edition of ChatGPT, DALL-E, Midjourney, or DeepSeek nullifies the protection we just gained. Like the never-ending task of updating computer virus profiles or patching a cybersecurity threat, the tools struggle to keep pace. So, what can we do that is not dependent on specific technology tools?

The answer is a durable process framework. When we encounter information, we need to consider the lessons we learned in earlier chapters about how we process, make judgments, and act. Becoming more deliberate takes time and requires a balanced investment between small and high-stakes decisions. Sharing a post about your favorite restaurant is a small decision. Decisions about your health or finances, however, are another matter.

However, each can benefit from the same approach, which starts with preempting our thinking rather than acting on basic instincts. Those basic instincts are driven by System 1 thinking, versus the slower, rational thinking of System 2. The process is repeatable. It is something that can be done while standing in line getting coffee; it only takes a few minutes. Ironically, it *starts with a stop*.

Identify the mental shortcut. Stopping for a moment allows people to pause their reaction and recognize how it makes them feel. Reassuring, fearful, appreciative. Checking our emotions in the moment. Pausing to ask, "Are the feelings because what we are seeing is true or simply recognizable?" Seeing a message frequently makes the message feel *fluent.* We love fluent concepts, and our mind more easily accepts a message that does not tax our thinking too much. Since it does not need to expend any extra energy, it is easy to believe. Easy is good, but it might not be right. It can confirm a prior experience (confirmation bias) or feel familiar (illusory bias).

Purposefully engage rational thinking. Stopping just for a second, turning off our first impulsive thoughts, and engaging our rational mind is a pivot. Researchers believe that it requires more than a 20-second pause. Instead, they discovered that consciously justifying initial conclusions and learning about the most common cognitive biases beforehand were most effective. Justification is as simple as considering what pieces of evidence would disprove a statement, headline, or claim. What evidence is needed to tell a different story?

Research. In a process known as *lateral reading*, when people simultaneously look for the same information across multiple sources, their ability to identify misinformation significantly improves. A large-scale digital media literacy study concluded that sorting news misinformation using lateral reading improved their results by 66%. Techniques like reverse image searches and simple searches for similar headlines and text provide authenticity.

Trace. In a world with billions of websites, news organizations, millions of posts on X/Twitter, Facebook, etc., and countless academic and government sources, there should be some reference to the original information. Who created it? When the source is not obvious, we need to be skeptical.

Tracing involves both finding the source artifact (e.g., picture, article, audio, etc.) and, more importantly, another element called source criticism. Source criticism is understanding what the artifact (picture, text, video) contributes. Verifying that a photo exists and is real does not necessarily support the accompanying narrative. For example, a picture of a celebrity walking beside someone outside a hotel is not evidence that the people were staying together at that hotel. Inspecting artifacts can also reveal what is missing. What is missing can be more important than what is shown.

A popular example circulated on many social media platforms in 2018. It was a picture of Prince William standing beside a car, apparently giving a middle-finger gesture to someone on the street. This was shocking and unexpected behavior for the prince. However, another photo from a different angle showed him standing next to the hospital, which completely changed the narrative. He was holding up three fingers, indicating his third child had just been born.

The narrative is an interpretation of an artifact by someone—a journalist, your neighbor, a complete stranger. Accept that no one is perfectly neutral. There are three things to examine:

1. Does the person present an interpretation beyond mere facts?
2. Do they reasonably explain *why* they interpreted the artifact in the way that they do?
3. Do they reflect on their interpretation, and are they *transparent* about their biases or prior experiences? Someone who shares that they have "seen something like this before" is not providing evidence. They are providing bias.

Journalists tend to be better at this, while *influencer-reporters* provide neither interpretation nor transparency. Frequently, they show a controversial topic hoping to generate engagement but do not add comments of their own. Like tossing a flame into a powder-keg room, they quickly leave the conversation rather than explain their rationale.

Kill the narrative. Narratives change when emotional adjectives are removed. What remains is hard data that is more consumable for our rational thinking. Judgment words are a common emotional device, especially important in social media. A post that is rewritten in bland language might be the best use of AI when browsing charged topics.

GenAI text, images, and videos, as good as they are today, are the worst they will ever be and will be exceptionally better in the future. Frameworks can aid our ability to avoid misinformation and malicious disinformation. They will slow the scroll, make us ask questions, seek alternative narratives, and be the most empowering thing we can do to benefit positively from GenAI online.

Steering the Algorithms

Your experience, perhaps your reality online, is strongly influenced by the algorithms that provide the "For You" type feeds. Instagram, Facebook, TikTok, and YouTube offer some ability for users to change their feed through settings and privacy options. Facebook does not explicitly give users the option to reset the algorithm but does allow control over content topics. You may also need to unfollow groups or people. Facebook can also track your activity *offsite*, meaning your online behavior when you are not using Facebook. There is also an option to disable this activity from showing you ads on Facebook for something you looked up somewhere else.

As described earlier, algorithms use your past online history to guide what to show you next. What if your hobbies and interests change over time? You have moved on, but the algorithms have not. TikTok specifically offers a For You Feed refresh. Another method is to seek new content by finding additional groups to follow and, where there is the option, choosing not to see certain content. As time goes on, eventually the algorithms get the hint, notice the change in your behavior, and shift content to something more engaging. While you might not be able to fully control the algorithms, you can sometimes nudge them in the right direction.

Currently, none of these countermeasures provided by the platforms address AI specifically. None. There are no controls for GenAI images or videos. No opt-out of AI-generated text or spurious news. It points to a blind recognition from social media platforms that they either do not see the need (customers are not yet demanding it) or they do not have the ability to monitor and control GenAI content on their sites. At the moment, it feels like there is little concern about the consequences of AI.

Early Morning

The verification moment in the new era of AI is important. That text message at 6:24 a.m. and the accompanying video can circumvent our senses, our rational thinking, and our judgment. The video shows a politician mocking her supporters. "They are so dumb, they will believe anything. . ." The frames show her slightly in and out of focus as someone is covertly filming with their phone. An unsteady image, but enough that you know it is her. It looks like her. It sounds like her. It is just so shocking to hear. But then you halt for those few seconds. Stop your irrational, biased thinking. Pause your innate emotional response.

You begin researching with some lateral reading of your own. A story this profound must be on every news source by now, but searching finds none among the popular sites. Why would the major networks not have this story at the top of every website with the words "Breaking News" in a red alert banner? You begin to trace the source and find that the images only appear on one site. The site looks authentic until you realize the title is a mesh of familiar newspaper names pasted together. Authentic in its appearance, but thin on content.

The video itself seems to have a story to tell. Its poor quality and low angle make it appear like covert footage. Taken without consent, without disclosure. The source is attributed to a reporter you have never heard of, and neither has the Internet when you search for other stories that they have written. None exist. You pause. Before you hit the share button, you realize it. This is AI. It is not real, only a real attempt to build doubt and disinformation.

The technology around this scenario, however, is real—and unregulated. ElevenLabs, Podcastle, and Resemble AI can clone voices using AI. Each is intended for legitimate business purposes, but each is another demonstration that *good* AI can also be used for bad. Another, Kling AI, focuses on developing AI videos. Its advanced motion-control feature allows users to create a video of themselves and then "kling" that image—their face and body—to another character, an anime character, or another *real* person. Video impersonation at an exquisitely high level of quality. All of these offer their services at a cost that would not even buy an hour of Hollywood studio time.

It is notable that the leading GenAI platforms do not provide the ability to generally detect the authenticity of AI artifacts. Google DeepMind SynthID, as described earlier, is an excellent beginning, but it does not work on anything that was created by other tools. In 2023, OpenAI briefly created an AI detector called RoBERTa for this purpose, but after six months it discontinued the effort due to too many false positives. In other words, it was too difficult to self-regulate the output of its AI tools. In a similar parallel, Facebook (Meta) also discontinued its authenticity efforts—it was too difficult, too expensive, and it caused false positives.

AI will continue to be pervasive in our mundane daily lives and ease into other high-stakes corners of our decisions. As its capabilities grow, so does the need for us to be protective of our own vulnerabilities. With government regulations lagging and intermittent self-governance that fails to be consistently trustworthy, our best defense for now is our own AI defense: standing in our own power and exercising our own agency for information sovereignty.

Key Takeaways

- AI detection tools are improving but remain imperfect. Blended uses of AI and human content make this even more challenging. Studies show that both humans and AI perform only slightly better than chance, making a single tool insufficient as your only AI defense.
- The AI arms race for content detection is real both among companies competing for viable business products and those that learn from those AI-detection tools to create further AI deception. AI adversarial models trained to evade detection can succeed against existing tools at rates above 78%.
- Verification frameworks can counter the AI arms races because they are not dependent on technology tools. Research, tracing, verification, and source criticism are a more durable approach to personal AI defense. Scalable solutions remain elusive.
- Social media, along with AI platforms, has mostly deferred AI authentication to third parties, news organizations, and individuals. Google DeepMind's SynthID is a worthy exception but requires such a high level of industry coordination that government regulatory involvement seems inevitable.

Notes

1. The California case was the largest fine to date. AI hallucinations in legal cases gather a lot of obvious attention, and there are likely many more AI impacts in other industries that are not required to be publicly documented. Researcher Damien Charlotin has assembled a database of legal AI hallucination cases, mostly occurring in the United States. `https://www.damiencharlotin.com/hallucinations`

2. In 1950, mathematician Alan Turing introduced the idea that a test could be devised to differentiate between a computer and a human. In his paper *Computing Machinery and Intelligence*, he conceived that technology could eventually have abilities that would rival human intelligence. The test involved an interrogator interacting with a computer and a human in a blind test. Referred to as the "imitation game," the interrogator judges responses from the computer and the human. When they cannot discern the difference, then the test is passed. This concept influenced and is demonstrated in the *Blade Runner* movies. `https://phil415.pbworks.com/f/TuringComputing.pdf`
3. Technical readers can find more details and a review of detection methods using various models.
   Arpan Mahara, and Naphtali Rishe. "Methods and Trends in Detecting AI-Generated Images: A Comprehensive Review." *arXiv* (2025). Last revised October 17, 2025. `https://doi.org/10.48550/arXiv.2502.15176`
4. Claiming AI-vs.-AI tools can be successful at high rates is unrealistic given the evolving nature of generative AI. Winston AI advertises 99.98% accuracy. TruthScan promotes 99%+ accuracy. GPTZero claims 99% accuracy.
5. Alexandra Fiedler, and Jörg Döpke. "Do Humans Identify AI-Generated Text Better than Machines? Evidence Based on Excerpts from German Theses." *International Review of Economics Education* 49 (2025): 100321. `https://doi.org/10.1016/j.iree.2025.100321`

Chapter 7

You Are the Target

Imagine right now, somewhere, someone you have never met is searching for the same thing you are online. It is a developing news story, and you are anxious for information. Same platform, same words, same moment, yet they are getting a different narrative than you. Not because they have wandered off to a fringe website, down a rabbit hole of misinformation, but because an algorithm has, in effect, been studying them for years—logging their clicks, likes, and shares; what they pause to view; and how long they linger. What they skip. What they don't. What they share with their friends. What they write in a comment. It reads the sentiment of those comments as negative, positive, reassuring, or angry.

These are data points to an algorithm that knows them better than most of their friends do. An algorithm that decided what version of the world each of them should see—the version they *prefer* to see. The algorithm is their invisible guide. But do not mistake this as something that happens to someone else. You have one too. You have had it for just as long, and it explains a lot about why two people in the same moment see two versions of the truth.

If you work with data, you may already know why. You understand recommendation engines, behavioral signals, and we have already discussed the concept of engagement optimization and why it is so important to platform providers. None of this is surprising—technically. What is more interesting is understanding how it plays out in real life. It is one thing to understand how a car is built and another to see it race down the highway. Understanding the mechanics is not the same as experiencing the journey of where that technology can go, especially when it is unrestrained—and customized just for you.

The Digital Twin You Never Met

Platforms see you in a very particular way. You are not a person to them. You are a behavioral model built in your own image, but built based on the *predictable* you. The you that is more likely to click on certain news articles, posts from influencers, and, most importantly, the buy button. It is not built to understand you or to get to know you in a way that is distinctly human. It is built to anticipate your next online step, and the best way to do this is to create a profile of you, your household, your family and friends, and all the interconnections that bridge between them. It is a data version of you, bound together with math. It is your digital twin.

Perhaps you consider yourself a social media nomad. You are not tied to any one social media platform. You might roam from one to the next without contributing posts or comments. Maybe you have an old-school approach altogether and have either never had a social media app or deleted your profile years ago. And while your contributions to a form of your digital twin might be sparse compared to those of 18–29-year-old women on Instagram (its most popular user type), it might surprise you that they are not completely zero. The reason is that nearly every U.S. household and most adults have some sort of profile maintained by social media platforms, even if those people do not use those apps.

It is a little like how scientists can detect that a planet exists and determine its specific chemical composition, not by directly observing it, but rather by observing other nearby objects. One planet near another can change its orbital gravity. The light reflected from a planet can indicate what it is made of because of its chemical signatures. With social media, you can also be observed indirectly without using a platform's app. In a 2018 U.S. congressional hearing regarding Facebook and social media privacy, Facebook's CEO revealed that Facebook collects data from people online even if they do not have a Facebook account. How?

Finding Your Friends

Platforms like Facebook and Instagram offer convenient tools to "Find Your Friends" and "People You May Know." In the guise of creating social communities, these tools allow you to upload your contacts and even automatically sync them with your mobile device. Conveniently, these tools can be used to begin a profile of a nonuser. They can also help the platforms match other data using email addresses. The additional data is obtained from unrelated sites that those nonusers might have visited, leaving trails of information that are collected and shared with data brokers.

For people who deliberately engage with a platform, most platforms allow you to download your own information, but there is something missing from that data. They do not explain *how* it is used by multiple algorithms to provide you with content, including advertising, or how you are connected to others in your social community. This is not unique to Facebook. Other platforms, in the name of data privacy and transparency, tout their willingness to offer users the ability to download and see their own data, but they are holding back a very important part of your online persona.

They will show you all the comments you have added, all the photos you have uploaded, and the devices and IP addresses you have used to access their platform. What is missing is the additional data. The things they know about you that you did not specifically add when you set up your profile. The data they filed under your name without your knowledge.

For most of us, it is the aggregated data from multiple sources that helps them model your preferences better than anything you explicitly share. Everything from your political stances and interests to your community of friends. It all becomes part of your larger digital profile. What insights might they know about you? Would this be interesting to share with you? The concern—what if they are incorrect?

Perhaps at this point you are wondering why this matters. Younger people who have grown up with technology are digitally fluent. Data privacy and the incursion of technology into their personal lives may not be concerning. Likewise, those data professionals working in these companies have a similar view that there is a certain acceptable trade-off between privacy and convenience. It is not entirely without consent, right?

Every platform and app has a privacy policy. You have seen it before—that Accept and Agree button most of us subconsciously check when we are signing up.[1] Those privacy agreements are important. They are also often impossible to read and understand, with many of them being *thousands* of words long. In the United States, most states allow companies to use, share, or sell any data they collect from you without notifying you when they do so. They can collect as much data about you as they want, provided they offer you a privacy policy disclosure and you have agreed. Further, when they do share your information with a third-party data broker, those third parties do not need to notify you either when they resell it to someone else. There exists a data ecosystem of information that you might be entirely unaware of, and it profits from your identity.

All this data that can form a digital version of you can feel intrusive, and it should, but what is the real harm, and how is this any different from an old-fashioned phonebook of decades gone past or your credit report? We accept in our society that some information about us is somewhat public. The issue is not about the information;

it is about the aggregation and its unexpected use. Less of a concern a decade ago, more now in the AI era. Let's consider a few ways a digital replica of you can be used.

Marketing analysis for generations has been about targeting people and predicting their responses. The past behavior of customers and others with similar demographics gives insights into their future behavior. A database of customers, along with attributes and past purchases, has become a statistical trove of understanding. Sophisticated models run by companies with large resources and deep talent could gain a competitive advantage. In the past, it was more about forecasting outcomes on a generalized basis and for large marketing segments. Those cohorts drove decisions about advertising spending along with story or product placements. Modeling large groups was a limitation of the data and computational power. With AI, this all changes. AI can not only model the behavior of a crowd of people in a probabilistic way; it can also model *your* behavior in a very deterministic way. Using your digital twin as a stand-in and creating an AI simulation becomes more about what you *will* do.

AI provides scale in a way that traditional marketing could never. In the past, bottlenecks were human creativity and costs. A brand could only afford to test-market a small number of variations of their ads developed by a limited creative team. A focus group of prospective customers could only discuss a fixed number of ideas before participants grew tired and the day grew short. Real people with real physical limitations. GenAI is boundless by comparison. It can generate novel concepts beyond the capacity of one or many creative teams, both in volume and perhaps even imagination. Instead of testing five or ten variations, it can experiment with thousands against the predictable responses of digital twins.[2] AI opens a door to hyper-personalization and profound efficiency for marketing, content design, and the very information we rely upon and trust.

While AI might arguably improve some of our online experiences by getting to know us better, there is another example of the danger of digital twins—fraud. While cyberattacks have continued to rise, there has been a notable inflection point following the launch of ChatGPT. Enabled by GenAI, McKinsey reported that the number of phishing attacks increased 138% from 2022 to 2023. Deloitte Center for Financial Services projects that GenAI-related losses in financial services alone could grow to $40 billion by 2027, a nearly threefold increase from 2023.

In 2025, Anthropic disclosed research that Claude had been used to orchestrate a sophisticated cyberattack campaign. The attackers used AI to develop code and autonomous AI agents to execute infiltrations at scale. They reported, ". . .the AI made thousands of requests, often multiple per second, an attack speed that would have been, for human hackers, simply impossible to match." AI can exploit systems rapidly at a time when IBM reports that the average response time to a cyberattack is 73 days. Days, not hours or minutes. Like the AI detection tools we discussed earlier, AI cybersecurity tools are also an antidote in an AI versus AI race. But there remains a weaker link in AI cybersecurity, and that is the human factor.

Humans in the loop for AI systems feel comforted by having a way to check the work of this new technology and to avoid mistakes. It can also be a vulnerability. In a well-publicized event in 2024, a British multinational company named Arup transferred $25 million to fraudsters. The scam unfolded when an employee first discounted a suspicious phishing email but was later asked to join a video conference call with the company CFO and others. It was exactly how a suspicious email might be cleared with an in-person conversation. During the call, the participants clarified and further requested a money transfer, and the employee complied. However, all the people on the video call, including those he recognized, were AI deepfake images and AI-cloned voices, each assembled from a digital twin.

Certainly, large companies and financial institutions will be at the forefront of AI defenses, and the story of Arup will be less likely to repeat. There is a first-mover advantage in cyberattacks that helps us prepare for similar security challenges. However, small and mid-sized organizations may not have the same abilities or awareness to keep pace with AI and will continue to be the most targeted. Strategy leaders in these institutions have an urgent need to understand their AI vulnerabilities. For the rest of us, AI twins can be used to target us or those in our social circles. Relative-in-need scams and romance traps will continue to proliferate and succeed with greater accuracy. With greater authenticity. They will know you. They will know your digital twin, and you have a right to know them too. We will discuss how regulation can help with the latter, but first we need to explore how we are experiencing the effects of AI and our deep-twinning profiles.

Personalized Reality Machine

> *"Me and only me, and maybe a few other people like me who agree with me."*
>
> —Anonymous

Step back for a moment to circa 1990 in New York City. You are standing in front of a newsstand on a busy street as people hurriedly step up, grab their favorite newspaper, pay the attendant, and move on. There are more than a dozen newspapers to choose from, not just from New York City but also from other cities, like the *Los Angeles Times*, the *Toronto Star*, and *The Times*. There is *The Wall Street Journal* next to the *New York Post*. There are the bellwethers of investigative journalism stocked next to the tabloids. It is an analog version of a social media news feed, but with a distinct difference.

As you stand there, you can see many different headlines, or rather many of the same stories with different takes on the news of the day. Each aligned with the paper's typical readers or perhaps varying due to the talents of individual reporters. One major event could be covered by all the newspapers, but few would have the exact same headline. You will also notice that the stories of the event carry many of the same facts but vary in their narratives. And this is exactly how it is different from social media today. It is diverse. The viewpoints are broad, overlapping, even contradictory, and you can easily see this all at once. You also have a choice. Grabbing two papers at the same time might seem like a waste of money for the same news, but it also gives you something more important—balanced information.

Invisible Feedback Loops

You are likely familiar with the term *echo chamber*. It is reminiscent of the idea of a large physical room where sound echoes off barren walls, bouncing from one to the next. Metaphorically, it is more often associated with the early days of social media chat rooms as places where people could talk about specific topics and common interests. Today it refers to how algorithms drive what we see and what we read. Unlike those chat rooms and old newsstands, we have limited choice about the information we encounter. Entering a chat room, we choose to *filter* the topics and ideas. Algorithms remove that deliberate choice, subjecting us to less diverse information. They run automatically, constantly learning our preferences, constantly building our digital twins, and constantly serving us predictable information that plays off our confirmation bias. We see what we want to see. We read what we want to read.

Several studies confirm this echo chamber effect, and it is more complex than just one person creating a message and others endlessly resharing it. In a study of Facebook content, researchers found that algorithms reduced exposure to diverse content by 15%, meaning that the data individuals provided in their profiles and their behavioral history narrowed what they saw online. Unknowingly. Their view of the newsstand is incomplete.

This is not surprising by itself. What is more surprising is that a person's engagement with the already limited content further reduced their exposure by 70%, suggesting that what a person does with that news—user selection—*dominated* the algorithmic effect. The algorithms were shaping the list of information, and then users' choices were *training and reinforcing* the algorithm. The echo, the rattling around of similar information that succumbed to our confirmation bias, was real.

The same study found that this was not uniform for all people. The narrowing of content and ideas was amplified by another factor. Those with strong political leanings in one way or the other were most likely to *not be exposed* to cross-cutting content. Your strong political opinions are reinforced by AI with repeated strong opinions.

People using different platforms experience the echo effect in varying degrees based on each platform's goals. For example, Meta (Facebook, Instagram, WhatsApp) and TikTok are focused on engagement—keeping you online as long as possible, sharing recurring themed content to build your digital twin and generate revenues. Other platforms such as X/Twitter encourage dialogue among users and are more likely to show cross-cutting content. Diverse ideas can cause debate and engagement in another way that still keeps you on their platform. Topic-focused services with fewer social connections, such as Reddit, can be even better for those who want to find differences in opinions. For their users, there is an active choice to opt into a topic thread in a way that is different from other social media platforms.

The consequences of personalization are driven by the motivation of platform providers, our digital twin profiles, and, of course, the choices we make in engaging with topics. The interplay of these three factors is important. It can fundamentally change how we see the world and, more importantly, how we see each other. One news event can be characterized differently depending on how our digital twin is determined to react.

A Newsstand of Information

Back to the circa-1990 newsstand. One of the top stories of that era was the arrest and murder trial involving O.J. Simpson. Standing there on the street in New York, you would have noticed the many newspapers and magazines covering the story and its lengthy trial. Side by side, you could, in that very analog way, *scroll* across the collection of publications before you made your choice. Looking at the June 27, 1994, magazine covers of *Newsweek* and *Time* might make you pause. Same story, same arrest photo of O.J. Simpson, but something strikingly different: *Time* magazine, with the headline "An American Tragedy," showed the picture dramatically darker, ominous, and almost sinister. The alteration of the photo was editorial judgment, although the end of the trial was more than a year away. Side by side, you could make your own judgment. You have agency and choice and can clearly see the narrative differences between *Newsweek* and *Time*. You can choose which to pick up and read and which to ignore.

News from social media feeds does not work like the newsstands of the past. We do not see alternative perspectives as much as we may want, nor do we know when we are seeing the judgmental and skewed versions of the news. This is the most important part. We do not always know why our "For You" news feeds look the way they do. *Newsweek* and *Time* made it obvious because many people could see their differences in plain sight. In our virtual reality echo chambers, it requires more effort, which is one of the goals of this book—to help us all understand the consequences of AI and enable us to be more conscientious consumers of the truth. But it will not be easy. Take the case of the arrest of Nekima Levy Armstrong in January 2026.

Shortly after her arrest for protesting at a church, a photo of her was published on X/Twitter, handcuffed and being escorted by a police officer. A standard photo given the moment, with Ms. Levy calm and composed as she walked. Later in the day, another post showed the *same* photo except her skin was darkened, her face was distraught, and she appeared to be crying. Judgment in an image. It was not real. *The New York Times* investigated and found they could easily replicate the photo manipulation using any of the popular AI image tools and a simple prompt. No expertise, just malicious intent. What they also revealed was shocking. Both photos, the real one and the AI crying photo, were posted by official agencies of the U.S. government. Hours apart from seemingly trustworthy sources. Government sources deliberately using AI. Depending on your digital twin, you likely only saw one. Your version of the truth was customized just for you.

Data Ecosystem Beyond the Feed

Like all ecosystems, the digital one needs something to feed it, and that something is data. Lots of data. It is estimated that there are currently 175 to 200 zettabytes of data in the world, and that number will likely double every 5 years.[3] It is difficult to measure how much of this is personal data shaping your online experiences, but to give some perspective, a study estimated that 70% of the world's population has data collected about them. Where does all this data come from? Meet the data brokers.

Data brokers collect, sell, and aggregate personal data about individuals and households. In the United States, leading firms like Acxiom claim to have records on 2.6 billion people across the globe, processing 1.2 trillion data records monthly, and gather more than

10,000 unique data points per individual and household.[4] In the United States, Acxiom has data on 260 million individuals, which is equivalent to the *entire* U.S. adult population. There are perhaps a thousand or more data brokers; however, only a few U.S. states require that they register with regulators, leaving the numbers unknown. There are 750 registered in California. Many of the larger companies are familiar, including the major credit bureaus and social media companies. Others may only be known to readers working directly in marketing. For companies, data brokers are ideally used to supplement the information they already have on their customers. Often, in exchange, those companies share customer information with brokers, who then in turn can also share or sell information to other brokers.

Collecting your information can be obvious in many examples—you fill out a form, sign up for a service, and you are in a database. It is direct and deliberate. Other methods of data collection are less transparent, and that includes website pixels and cookies. We are all familiar with cookies and those mandated pop-ups requiring us to accept or decline their use when we visit a website. Cookies can be convenient when you return to a retail site and your cart still contains the items you selected, keeping you logged in.

Although cookies can be used to define your online profile, they are more known than pixels. Pixels are the familiar parts of a digital image, but in the context of tracking you online, they have been repurposed. Many websites have code that references images from other sites, but these pixels have no intention of returning a real image. Instead, they send information about you (e.g., products you viewed, IP addresses, device information, and timestamps) to data brokers. The moment you visit a site or click on a subpage, hundreds of tiny pixel messages travel to other servers.[5] It is how marketers and their product offers can follow you across the internet. An item you just viewed on Wayfair can appear instantly in an offer when you open Facebook. But could knowing which websites you visit really be useful for defining your digital twin?

An analysis published in *Scientific Reports* in 2025 showed that an individual's browsing behavior can act like a digital fingerprint. Merely visiting four websites was enough to uniquely identify 95% of individuals. This was not a result of a small-study coincidence. The study included over 2,000 participants and tracked 9 million website visits across 49,000 domains. While we might believe we are different from others, this shows how data can feed deterministic algorithms with high accuracy. Every time you visit a website, you create a trail of information—where you journeyed from and where you are going. While we can decline cookies and use browser extensions to block pixel scripts, we are left with little ability to prevent the detection of website-browsing fingerprints. Efforts to create privacy protections for one method only seem to create opportunities for data brokers to discover novel new methods to navigate around those protections. Why are they so persistent?

The data-broker business is a $140 billion revenue industry where market leaders are showing double-digit growth. The industry is being lifted by GenAI. The development of AI agents that can automate the collection of individual data supplements the physical capabilities of data researchers, making profiles deeper and more complete. Researchers who spend days or weeks assembling data from disparate sources can have multiple AI agents complete these tasks in minutes.

GenAI is also building digital twins of your digital twin in a process called *synthetic data generation*. With a more complete view of you by harvesting your real information, data brokers can use AI to create other versions of you with slight variations. It is the equivalent of sampling your DNA, changing a portion of it, and then testing to see how it responds in a lab. Synthetic data can be used to test products and create consumer simulations, all while side-stepping data privacy laws that strictly rule on your *personal* data, not replicated data. The data ecosystem remains robust, and AI only gives it more depth.

A Different Worldview

The previous sections discussed the mechanisms—the profiles, the data brokers, and how our own behavior contributes information. The proverbial gears and wheels that are in motion. Too many to individually manage. Too distributed to centrally regulate. They have an ecosystem of their own that is interdependent, and perhaps unstoppable. We may be able to slow some parts through our personal defenses—our awareness, our actions—only to find that another piece of the industry has navigated around us. When we are the target, how can we both participate and remain invisible?

There are consequences at scale, and we are historically subjected to more influence by AI than ever. A targeted product offering, a targeted story, even a targeted reality. AI can either craft the images, or the narrative, or simply use what it knows about us to craft the unfolding of information and news that we see. In some regards, AI is helpful in finding what matters most to us individually; however, we need transparency when AI is less informative, when it is too eager to give us only what we want. There may be times when we really do want to see opposing perspectives and ideas. This is not yet a feature of social media, likely because it brings the risk of disengagement. AI may lose track of us if we go off on another track of exploration, a most human trait of individual growth. We might stop scrolling, get bored, and simply log off.

Different worldviews are surprisingly possible even when we are all tuned into the same source of information. The proverbial newsstand of the past is not a window into the events of the day, but a narrowed one, without recognition, without notice. And while we are not locked into our own echo chambers, there are times when it feels like we are hidden from outside voices. Except for major news stories, our just-for-you feeds remain that—just for you and only you, with no two alike. We may find comfort in this at times when the outside world is less comfortable. We may also never see beyond our current perspectives and understandings of the world around us.

Isolation and loneliness are a consequence of not only how we get information but also *who* we get information from. Interactions with other people—friends and strangers alike—can help us see a broad range of ideas. But AI, our digital twin, and the algorithms, if they were conscious, would feel abandoned, perhaps threatened by our independence from them for a moment. Daring to explore, take a different route to work from that offered by Google Maps, choose an alternative news source (a paper newspaper if you can find one), or buy the least recommended product online (those not sponsored), gives us that different worldview.

It is the one challenge you need to explore starting today. The algorithms will forgive you.

Key Takeaways

- You have a digital twin you did not create. We all do. Platforms build behavioral profiles of you using every click, share, and comment, along with public records and personal device data, including your location.
- Your data profile exists even if you have opted out. Through others' contact uploads, third-party data brokers, cookies, pixel tracing, and your unique browser footprint, platforms

(*continued*)

(*continued*)

can build a profile of you without your knowledge or permission.

- Algorithms and your own choices narrow your worldview. Studies show that algorithms reduce your exposure to diverse information by 15%, and your own engagement with what is provided further reduces cross-cutting content by 70%.
- Data brokers aggregate your information and have extensive coverage across the globe. In the United States, most of the adult population is profiled through data collection, sharing, and reselling of your information in an industry that faces few regulatory hurdles.
- GenAI has supercharged both the creation and exploitation of your digital twin, from hyper-personalized advertising to deepfake fraud schemes.
- When AI guides what we see and read, two people can experience an event in very different ways. AI can not only change how we see the world; it can also change how we see each other. Your beliefs and the version of the truth you are presented with are really only what algorithms allow you to see unless you actively research different perspectives.

Notes

1. A Brookings Institution study found that most people (72%) rarely read the terms of service when signing up for online services. This is likely driven by time constraints and the very lengthy and ambiguous nature of privacy policies. `https://www.brookings.edu/articles/brookings-survey-finds-three-quarters-of-online-users-rarely-read-business-terms-of-service`

2. Unilever, the company behind brands like Dove and TRESemmé, has developed digital twins of its products to rapidly create multiple versions of its advertising. The company reports a 55% savings in production and 65% faster turnaround on content creation, in addition to boosting product desirability and bringing products to market. `https://www.unilever.com/news/news-search/2025/unilever-reinvents-product-shoots-with-ai-for-faster-content-creation`
   Panoplai is a market research company that offers customer digital twins for marketing brands to use interactively. AI as an alternative to human focus groups can be appealing, reducing costs and time. However, like all data models, the accuracy of the digital twin drifts over time and requires continual updating as consumer preferences change. `https://www.panoplai.com/digital-twins`
3. This is simply an estimate based on data from Statista and the IDC Global DataSphere forecast. Readers of my previous book, *Data Duped*, will know that this is often an elusive measure. Sources vary in their estimates, and their methodology is often built on the estimates of others. The research has its limitations, and the point in referencing it here is not to be exact but to suggest that the data available is both difficult to put into relatable terms and growing at a rapid pace. `https://www.statista.com/statistics/871513/worldwide-data-created`
4. The number of attributes tracked is not the same as the number collected. For many individuals, some attributes are missing. However, Acxiom does not disclose the completeness of individual and household records.
5. The use of pixel scripts varies by the type of website. Retailers and news sites tend to have more, while healthcare organizations and governments tend to have fewer. The number of pixels can range from a few to hundreds. Google AdSense and Meta Pixel are the two most deployed, and it is reported that Google maintains a tracking presence on 80.3% of all websites. Meta Pixel is used on 18.7% of the top one million websites.
   Kyungmin Sim, Honyeong Heo, and Haehyun Cho, "Combating Web Tracking: Analyzing Web Tracking Technologies for User Privacy," *Future*

Internet 16, no. 10 (2024): 363, https://doi.org/10.3390/fi16 100363
Paschalis Bekos, Panagiotis Papadopoulos, Nicolas Kourtellis, and Michalis Polychronakis, "PIIxel Leaks: Passive Identification of Personally Identifiable Information Leakage through Meta Pixel," in *Proceedings of the 2025 ACM SIGSAC Conference on Computer and Communications Security (CCS '25)* (New York: Association for Computing Machinery, 2025), 4229–43, https://doi.org/10.1145/3719027.3765113

Chapter 8

Community and Collective Intelligence

Our Shared Reality

On the morning of July 17, 2014, noted AIDS researcher Dr. Joep Lange sat with his partner, Jacqueline van Tongeren, aboard Malaysian Flight 17, leaving from Amsterdam and bound for Kuala Lumpur. Down the aisle, Indiana University doctoral student Karlijn Keijzer, who was studying chemistry and treatments for Alzheimer's disease, arranged her things as she cleared her mind of her studies to welcome her vacation. Nearby, Cor Schilder and his girlfriend, Neeltje Tol, were looking forward to taking a break from the flower shop they owned in Volendam to see the sights in Bali. With their destination in mind, they gave little thought to what would happen on their journey.

Several hours after takeoff, while transiting Ukraine at an altitude of 33,000 feet, their plane suddenly tore apart.

For the 298 passengers and crew, their lives abruptly ended. What would begin next was a struggle for explanation, a search for truth, intertwined with politics and conspiracy.

Most stories like these quickly appear in our news feeds. The most basic facts, time and place, are then followed by more in-depth investigative reporting and government inquiries. Eliot Higgins read the story on his computer as he sat far from its location in Leicester, England. He was not a journalist, at least not in the traditional sense. The news of MH17 captured his attention. He had experience researching other obscure news stories, such as hidden parts of the Syrian war, which he posted on his blog in his spare time.

The blog gained attention from some journalists who referenced his information. He knew he was onto something, and a few days before the crash of MH17, he started a UK-based group of online journalistic detectives that he called Bellingcat. Bellingcat was fittingly named for a fable about mice who attempt to tie a bell to a cat that would warn them of danger. Soon Higgins set to work with his group of volunteers to crowdsource images from the crash and to try to figure out what had happened.

The investigation of the crash by traditional resources was marred from the very start. The airline was based in Malaysia, departed from the Netherlands, where most of the passengers were from, and the crash occurred over Ukraine. Ukrainian air traffic control guided the aircraft through its airspace, along with others that day, despite the nearby hostilities of Russian-backed separatists. The crash site was 50 km from the Russian border. The Netherlands led a joint investigative team but required coordination with other countries. This required time, diplomacy, ground resources, and effort, and soon stalled when authorities in the United States, Ukraine, and Russia traded accusations about who was responsible.

How could a plane just fall out of the sky while at cruise altitude? It is the least likely time for a fatal accident, and Higgins began focusing on what they did have.[1] The official investigations, locating and deciphering the "black box," would take months. What they did have was social media, those comments and, most importantly, pictures and videos shared by individual civilians following the crash. It was the beginning of what Higgins described as the "digital breadcrumb" trail of evidence. In those videos, Higgins and his team spotted images of a Buk missile system—portable launching systems that are deployed on mobile truck units. The Buk was located unexpectedly in Ukraine at the time of the crash. Using open-source tools like

Google Maps, Google Earth, and purchased satellite images from DigitalGlobe, they were able to geolocate the pictures and trace the movements of the Buk missile system back to its original location—a Russian military base in the town of Kursk.

The investigation was fueled by a community of online volunteers who analyzed clues in the background of pictures, such as trees, power lines, and billboards. An important finding while they tracked the missile platform's movements was the revelation that it was missing one of its four missiles the day after Flight MH17 fell out of the sky.

The Russian Ministry of Defense steadfastly denied responsibility and publicly provided contrary evidence placing blame on Ukraine. The Netherlands Joint Investigation Team (JIT) soon began following the work of the community, which was shared publicly and transparently on its website, explaining its process and conclusions. The JIT, along with its additional intelligence data, was able to refute all the counterclaims and, in a court hearing in 2022, charged several individuals in connection with the deaths of the passengers and crew.[2]

The volunteers intuitively discovered how to find small details of meaning in the evidence they could gather on their own or learned these skills by attending the many Bellingcat workshops. A new generation of investigative journalists had been introduced, driven by curiosity and the thrill of the hunt for truth. They were motivated in the same way as journalists, but they pursued answers part-time, in collaboration, where one person might have part of the puzzle that could then be handed off to the next person to dig deeper. From its roots as a scrappy Kickstarter project to its current form as an asset for journalists, Bellingcat started a trend where amateurs could help solve mysteries.

In the case of Flight MH17, the JIT had the same publicly available information as Bellingcat, perhaps even more considering their intelligence agencies, than open-source investigators could ever touch. But it was the crowd that accurately told the story first. Bellingcat's success at leveraging the efforts of an online crowd of investigators proved to be more agile at sifting through evidence. At a time when there are fewer journalists and an even smaller number of traditional news outlets, giving agency to individuals may be our best hope.

The Limits of Centralized Control

Big Brother. The Wizard of Oz. The Oracle of Delphi. God. Saraswati. There is a reason these archetypes and characters recur in mythology, religion, and fiction. We all want to know the truth. The absolute truth. And while we know some truths to be self-evident, others are more elusive and require that we either independently or collectively seek them out. It would be too easy for us to be provided with "obvious" facts, but what might be self-evident to one may not be to another, because facts by themselves are not answers; they are simply data. Data needs interpretation and context. It requires removing the noise, sifting through what remains, and applying critical thinking to obtain something useful. Without building collective wisdom and individual skills, all that is left is to consult our oracles for answers, which has limitations of its own.

As discussed earlier, as a society, we seek information from many centralized sources, including governments, academia, and news organizations. But trust in these traditional sources of information is shifting and being displaced by other centralized sources in the form of social media. The problem with centralization is the volume of information that one needs to sift through to find something useful.

Imagine you are one of 160 million tax filers in the United States. Few things can feel more complicated than taxes, no matter where you live in the world. You have a question. You need an answer. You need the truth, and your tax bill or refund is on the line. One option is to call the IRS help line, which in each of the past three years has received 100 million calls—and this is after nearly five times as many people have visited the IRS website. GenAI chatbots are now answering 35 million of those calls. And the ones that AI and humans cannot get to are causing people to seek answers impatiently from other places.

While AI is not causing the increase in volume of calls to the IRS, it might be creating volume in other areas, namely on social media. Social media offers a solution to our urgent questions from taxes to healthcare. Where it may be short on accuracy it makes up for it in providing solutions—any solution.

Facebook reports that there are roughly one billion posts on its platform *daily*. Some posts are useful, some are not, and others are misinformation. In part to rebuild goodwill with users, Facebook began collaborating with third-party fact-checkers in 2016 and increased its efforts in 2018 following the Cambridge Analytica fallout.

Facebook partnered with nearly 30 organizations to check content, but given the volume, it required an effective strategy focusing on only the most viral content or content that explicitly violated its policies. Once an item was flagged, it was used to flag other similar content. In most cases, the content was not deliberately removed, but rather it was deemphasized in Facebook's algorithms. It was still available to some, less available to others. Somewhere at the end of the scroll, someone could still see it.

The overall volume was comparatively small. In 2024, Facebook in the EU fact-checked 150,000 articles that were used to label or reduce the virality of over 27 million pieces of content. By early 2025 Meta announced that it was discontinuing the use of third-party content verification across all it US platforms, including Facebook. It was a nod toward the scale of the community verifiers that the platform could not otherwise solve. The availability of knowledgeable researchers was less of a factor than volume. Facebook has become a successful product spanning a larger number of people around the globe, and its users have a lot to share, which was just too much for Meta to keep up with.

One challenge with professional fact-checking groups like `FactCheck.org`, PolitiFact, Snopes, and AFP Fact Check, among others, is that they are remarkably like traditional news organizations. They are journalists, and some of them, like PolitiFact, trace their roots to newspapers. Their processes, attention to detail, and unbiased policies are the same. This is generally good because those professionals have content expertise and outperform crowdsourced fact-checking on more complex, in-depth topics. Their subject matter expertise gives them broader context beyond just verifying what was said (the source) to understanding what it means (the context).

Professional fact-checkers also have a complicated relationship with some readers. Their association with newspapers, even their presentation as a source, makes people not trust them. There is an increased level of distrust in journalists. Some believe there are agendas or stories they just are not willing to tell. Some believe they are *hiding* the truth, which makes skeptics of professional fact-checkers.

For skeptics, the work of professional fact-checkers can backfire, inadvertently raising belief in something they are disproving. Giving attention to a false claim helps broadcast it farther to a larger audience, who, as skeptics, see some truth among the fabrications.

Community notes describe the growing trend of crowdsourced fact-checking that most large social media platforms have adopted. You likely have seen these attached to a post, where others have added context in the form of a short note and you are asked to rate it. These are useful, and research has shown that posts that are flagged with a community note have 36% few reposts, meaning that they are effective at limiting the propagation of misinformation. Community notes add a type of friction that not only slows down reposts but, by removing poor content, also improves the overall quality of information on platforms. Unlike third-party fact-checkers used by Facebook, which would throttle the spread of a post in its algorithm or remove it, community notes generally do not directly change the platform's distribution of the post.

Community posts work on consensus, which sounds like a good idea, but they also have some limitations. Notes are written and voted upon by users known as contributors. While we are all members of the community, most contributors require approval by the platforms, which is the first limitation. Platforms share a similar intent, although their implementations are inconsistent. Their gate-keeping practice of only allowing verified users to be contributors is intended to thwart malicious or biased annotations from tipping the scale of accuracy. Verification, of course, is necessary, but by making the process of becoming a contributor more difficult, fewer potential contributors will step forward. The next limitation is that not all notes are shared with the public for voting.

The Washington Post has reported that only about 20% of community notes created on X/Twitter are eventually shared. The reason is that a community note requires other contributors with different views (such as political leanings) to agree on the *quality* of the note. It is not a simple majority vote of contributors, but a majority vote of different types of contributors. It requires people with opposing ideologies to agree.

You can likely see the problem with this, and it can create a truth void. When a post is polarizing and none of the contributors from the other side comment on it, then the initial note will *never* be shown to the public for a "that was useful" vote by regular members of the platform. Misinformation can persist, not because of a lack of debate, but rather because no one really wanted the debate. Posts seemingly so ridiculous that they do not warrant a response go unnoted. All of this persists without transparency. Users do not see notices of pending community notes, and it demonstrates perhaps the greatest flaw in how community participation can otherwise reduce misinformation.

One of the more obvious limitations of centralized information controls is gatekeeping. While *The New York Times*, the World Health Organization, the Louvre, and even your local public library all have good intentions to provide us with knowledge, they also gatekeep that knowledge. Gatekeepers decide how information is curated. *The New York Times* can only write about a constrained number of stories, limited by the capacity of its journalists. How it decides to prioritize who, what, where, and when to report is a form of gatekeeping. Your local library has similar constraints on its collections and requires patrons to visit its physical building. In its digital incarnation, access is broader but still limited to the information that it chooses to provide and often limited only to patrons who can demonstrate they live within the community.

Social media has promise, like the Internet, to bring information to the masses, and when properly verified can be as useful as traditional sources. Of course, social media is not designed solely to be an information source, but as it increasingly functions as one, responsibility follows function. The platforms are no longer just passive conduits of information displaying all posts equally in time order like a 1990s group chat. They actively choose via their algorithms what people see or do not see, and as those navigators, they have an obligation to steer you away from misinformation and propaganda.

However, there is another type of gatekeeping at risk, which is the control structure of social media. Meta (Facebook/Instagram) is majority-controlled by founding CEO Mark Zuckerberg, X/Twitter is essentially owned by Elon Musk, and TikTok USDS (the US entity) is owned by a small group of venture capital investors.[3] The nature of their ownership makes them less accountable to a corporate board or shareholders and allows them to be influenced directly by a small group of owners. This in contrast to Reddit, which is a public company, and Wikipedia, which operates as a nonprofit organization.

Promise and Hope in Crowdsourced Verification

In 2019, Oli Blake sat in the contestant's chair of the UK version of the game show *Who Wants to Be A Millionaire?* The progressive nature of the show allows the contestant to answer trivia questions and, with each question, move closer to winning 1 million pounds. Blake was playing well, having reached 125,000 pounds, but he was stuck on a question. He had narrowed it down to one of two possible answers. He knew, like many of us who might have been to corporate leadership training, that groups of people can solve problems better than individuals alone. He turned to the group in the studio and said he wanted to "Ask the Audience." The question was about an opening phrase of a novel ("3 May. Bistritz. Left Munich at 8:35 P.M."), and the choices were A. *Tinker Tailor Soldier Spy* or *B. Dracula*. The audience overwhelmingly chose A, 81% to 19%. He likely knew that on the show the audience provided the correct answers 91% of the time. He agreed and locked in his answer—and in that moment, he lost 93,000.

The story of Oli Blake is rare. Most of the time, crowdsourcing information leads to better decisions. However, it requires certain conditions to be effective. As noted earlier, crowds can underperform subject matter experts. So, let's look at what factors make crowdsourcing work.

James Surowiecki's 2004 book, *The Wisdom of Crowds*, provides the argument that groups often make better decisions under four specific circumstances. These conditions are timeless and intuitive if you have had the experience of working with a good team.

People who have had the opposite experience of working with dysfunctional teams will know that the quality of the team begins with who is in the room and why these four conditions are important.

Diversity of knowledge: Members of the group have a wide, sometimes incongruent, set of information. Data professionals will recognize that this is when a team is composed of people with different work backgrounds and levels of experience. New people may know less about a topic but ask questions that challenge current assumptions. This can push a group into new directions and allow it to explore ideas thoroughly. Non-subject matter experts can help a team just as much as those who believe they already have the answers.

Independence: Members of the group need not be influenced by others, which will dilute their contributions. Staying independent is at the core of avoiding groupthink bias. Many of us have experienced groupthink unfold when we enter a room and the leader or someone else with a bigger voice than others begins commanding the decision rather than discussing the problem or opportunity. Others' points of view are minimized or never heard. Even when suppressing ideas is not intentional, participants in the group might doubt their own responses. Maybe they have it wrong or do not understand the context as much as everyone else. Their ideas get shaped by others inadvertently. One effective strategy to maintain independence is to have in-person participants write their ideas first before the group shares them. A thoughtful moderator is key to fostering inclusion.

Decentralization: Where independence is how you think about a problem or process, decentralization is about what you know. It allows participants to draw on their own knowledge rather than referencing a centralized, authoritative knowledge base. Examples of a centralized knowledge base include your company's detailed strategic plan or relying solely on one prescribed source of information, one website, or one database. Decentralization helps avoid gatekeeping and silos of information that might inhibit the best ideas and resulting decisions.

Aggregation: This gives the group structure and a mechanism to turn individual judgments into a collective decision. If the group is estimating the measurable outcome of an experiment, it is a method that can summarize and report the average expected results. No one person may know the exact answer but may well provide estimates within a reasonable range. For example, a group estimating the number of jellybeans in a jar, when averaging the guesses, will be right within 3% of the total.

In a professional setting, picture yourself in a conference room, and you might have witnessed a good example of the wisdom of crowds. It likely included all the preceding conditions, plus one more very important one: the leader. The leader is the person moderating the discussion and leading the topics. It adds hierarchy to the focus of the crowd, i.e., meeting participants, on a limited set of priorities. The leader gives direction, and the aggregation role is not only assembling the results of the group but also shaping them into recommendations and decisions.

This structural component is also what drives one of the most successful crowdsourced repositories of information, Wikipedia. While anyone can sign up to be an editor and choose any topic to edit, Wikipedia also has tools that direct the "crowds" to prioritized articles. These articles may be flagged by other editors or by Wikipedia's algorithms. Wikipedia offers training on how to edit and maintains standards that make the pages uniform, such as requiring links to reference materials. The English version of the site has more than 7 million pages, adding thousands each month. The site receives over 4 billion visits each month and is moderated by its 52 million registered users. Most do not act as editors, but there is a core of about 238,000 users who make monthly edits and 800 administrators.

Wikipedia began competing with traditional encyclopedias and soon surpassed them in volume, relevance, and accuracy. It is often referred to as an authoritative source and used by most GPT-like tools for training. Its open-source nature and nonprofit structure make it one of the most unbiased information resources. Wikipedia has also adopted a Neutral Point of View (NPOV) policy as one of its three guiding principles to reduce editorial bias. The other two policies are verifiability, requiring references to known sources, and no original research.

While Wikipedia might be more comparable to the Library of Alexandria in its scope to capture all knowledge, its success is proof that large groups of individuals working independently can create the best source of the truth. With more than 25 years of crowd-sourced wikis, it should not be a surprise that social media platforms are turning to this method to fact-check their sites. But is it possible to apply a Wikipedia-style approach to your social media feed?

Similar to centralized fact-checking, the biggest hurdle is volume. Wikipedia has 285,000 fact-checking monthly active authors (MAAs) and about 15,000 new articles per month. X/Twitter has 40,000 MAAs; however, there are many more posts. The platform displays roughly 500 million (yes, *million*) posts per day, about 5,800 per second. While an article on Wikipedia is much more in-depth than a short post on X/Twitter or Facebook, the difference in volume is orders of magnitude greater. This, of course, leaves doubt, given the current plans, about how the crowdsourcing MAAs can be most efficiently directed toward reviewing content.

As an example, in early 2025 Facebook abruptly discontinued formal fact-checking of posts in favor of crowdsourced community notes while using the balance of the year to implement community notes. This was effectively a blackout period for truth verification. The impact was stunning. During this time, most posts did not publicly get reviewed, with only 900 tagged with community notes in the first 6 months. Previously, the 80 professional fact-checking organizations that partnered with Facebook, flagged *35 million posts* in the EU alone. This was a foreshadowing that community notes seem less likely to be applied than their predecessor.

The intent is simple: social media platforms want to allow freedom for anyone (i.e., an approved community note contributor) to fact-check and add a community note to a post. A touted principle of the process is that no one person can influence the results, because an algorithm, not a person, decides when a community note is shared. Their emphasis on unbiased freedom is admirable. In practice, it may not be practical, and you can probably already see why. Those notes require agreement among people who do not usually agree on the content *they* see. Because those algorithms are supercharged on engagement, people with different views likely never see the same content, especially polarizing content. Different views and similar content are less likely to converge, and so is the community.

Another issue is specialization and expertise. Wikipedia both presents content that needs review using an algorithm and allows fact-checkers to find content in their domain of expertise. Some experimentation on X/Twitter is using an algorithm to create a short list of posts that need review; however, these are only selected when a post's notes are near the tipping point to be shared with a broader group of users. Allowing fact-checkers the ability to use tools and find content that makes the best use of their skills, background, and expertise is optimal.

Bellingcat is equally successful for the same reason. Its contributors can specialize in topics that match their expertise. Crowdsourced investigative journalism has hope, but does it also have limitations in the new AI era? As noted, nearly anyone can portray themselves as a citizen reporter with professional results (i.e., AI-generated fakes). An element that makes crowdsourcing work requires some organized direction and a hybrid of AI tools, content selection, and the leveraging of cohorts of experts.

The best approach for crowdsourcing misinformation is to look at the structures and relationships between organizations using the digital solidarity economy (DSE) framework. DSE challenges both the centralization of the information providers (i.e., social media platforms) and the consolidation of the approvers of truth. It considers the costs and resources required. In other words, economics guide the allocation and division of duties.

A successful case study is the Taiwanese civics-technology platform named Cofacts. Cofacts is a decentralized fact-checking organization. It operates similarly to Wikipedia, but rather than checking articles, it is embedded in a social media platform to check misinformation. It operates as a two-part duocracy model. There is no hierarchy and there is no assignment of tasks. At one level, individuals can identify items that need review. At the other, people who volunteer can freely choose which items they research and fact-check. There are no community votes or required algorithmic approvals of their responses. This is in contrast to US-based social media approaches.

To compare the three types of fact-checking approaches, first we need to start with social media. In the past, organizations like Meta and X/Twitter chose their fact-checking groups, and even in the present, when using community note-takers, they have influence on which information is fact-checked and shared with their general users. They have control. Their economic motives remain unchanged, focusing on revenue, and they are motivated to minimize any negatives resulting from fact-checking.

Second, third-party fact-checking organizations, like PolitiFact, operate like a nongovernmental organizations (NGOs). They are not as authoritative as the government itself but use a journalistic approach with a closed editorial process and no input from the public. They rely on grants and foundations and maintain independence.

Lastly, there are decentralized groups like Cofacts. Their anonymous volunteers and collaborative editing, like Wikipedia, provide an environment that is not influenced by large organizations with large financial incentives. They maintain the most independence. Their funding is minimal, as they seek free advice and donations.

Cofacts as an organization is unique and serves as a model for others. It is technically integrated with the LINE app, which is a messaging and social media platform popular in Taiwan, Japan, and Indonesia. App users flag items for review by Cofacts from within the app, reducing friction in fact-checking topics. On X/Twitter users can currently ask Grok to check a topic; however, Grok and X are part of the same company, and Grok lacks some independence.

The effort of decentralized verification continues, and it is not without hope and promise. While the scale of social media has outpaced the capacity (and trust) of third-party fact-checkers, new ideas fill in the gaps. The success of Bellingcat, Wikipedia, and Cofacts suggests that there is more work to be done to make social media platforms independent. However, while revenues are at stake, those changes may come with reluctance among a group of tightly held companies that have yet to see discord among their patrons. Certain conditions must prevail for this to be successful.

You may still be wondering why Oli Blake got it wrong. Groups can make errors. The risks of following the crowd sometimes mean going in the wrong direction. They could be missing wisdom, critical thinking, or, more dangerously, have malicious participants.[4] Picture the scenes of an out-of-control crowd, those rioting, or the torches and pitchforks mob chasing Frankenstein's monster, and you will get the idea. They may have succumbed to misinformation, or anger and fear that prevent us from more rational thinking. In the case of Blake, it was not bad actors but a lack of independence that led to groupthink bias.

On the show, recall that he had narrowed the answers to just two. A simple task for the crowd to pick between them. But before he asked the audience for help, he said something more important. "A. Tinker Tailor Soldier Spy seems plausible." He planted an idea, and the independence of the group was lost. Those who might have been feeling somewhat confident it was Dracula had a moment of doubt. No one wants to be wrong, so those who likely knew the right answer, paused and agreed with the crowd, and they were wrong.

When Collective Intelligence Fails

In April 2013, two days after the Boston Marathon bombing, social media crowds on Reddit were doing what they do best. They were sharing ideas, checking details, and piecing together fragments of information to identify what happened and who was responsible. The crowds moved faster than the journalists and even the FBI. Within hours they identified the bomber. Except they hadn't. The person they named was Sunil Tripathi, a college student at Brown University, who stopped attending classes a month earlier. His face was posted somewhere, or rather, many places in fact, as his family had set up a search for him. Someone saw the picture. Someone else connected a few possible dots. The journalists and authorities, taking a more measured approach, soon identified the real suspects two days later. For those couple of days, Sunil's family was overwhelmed when the crowdsourcing had both failed them in their search for him and, separately, in the search for the bombers.

Collective intelligence can work. It can also be twisted, manipulated, and at times take on a life of its own. Bad ideas can persist, right alongside good ones. It can self-correct, and even before the FBI's announcement, Redditors were questioning the conclusions of the crowd. In days, not weeks.

The failure of the wisdom of crowds is as old as the Salem witch trials of 1692. It is a human condition, but it is less likely to persist in the modern era. However, AI can complicate this process. There is almost instantly more information that needs to be reviewed, and the scale can limit the ability of crowdsourcing.

While more social media platforms are pivoting away from third-party fact-checkers to crowdsourcing at scale, a recent study showed that it is not as simple as substituting one for the other. The study looked at community notes on X/Twitter to understand the patterns between posts and approved community notes. What the researchers discovered was that when there was bilateral agreement among community contributors, it was when they could each reference a credible third-party fact-checked source.[5] This finding suggests that while platforms are reducing their investments in support of third-party fact-checkers in lieu of community crowdsourcing, it is those very third parties that are needed for the community to be successful. Without third parties, the community will lack unity and a common reference point for knowledge. When the community fails to agree, then the notes are invisible, and it will appear to most users that they are on their own to determine the truth from the noise.

Key Takeaways

- Crowdsourced verification works, but only under the right conditions. It can outperform individual judgment when there is diversity of knowledge, independence, decentralization, and a method of aggregation.
- Scale remains an unsolved problem. Professional third-party fact-checkers, platform moderation, and community note contributors all have limitations that cannot keep pace with the rapidly expanding amount of AI-generated misinformation.
- Community notes and fact-checking are not substitutes, but rather an interconnected mechanism. Community notes can serve as a rapid distribution system for the authoritative knowledge of third-party fact-checking and journalism.
- Platforms adopting community-notes approaches seek to reduce bias by requiring a balance of opinions. However, the opposite occurs, resulting in truth voids and a small number of notes shared with platform users. Misinformation persists.
- Decentralized models, exemplified by Wikipedia, Bellingcat, and Cofacts, provide governance structures that are the most promising paths forward. They must be organized, specialized, and structurally insulated from the economic pressures that compromise platform-based approaches.

Notes

1. Flight takeoffs and landings are the most dangerous phases of flights. Final approach and landing account for 46% of all fatal plane accidents. Fatal crashes during the cruising segment account for 9%. The leading

cause of all accidents is pilot or human error, linked to 60–80% of crashes in various studies. Mechanical failures are the next most likely cause, followed by weather-related crashes (www.faa.gov/sites/faa.gov/files/2023-10/statsum_summary_2022.pdf).

2. Three individuals were found guilty: Igor Girkin, Sergey Dubinskiy, and Leonid Kharchenko. Tried in absentia, they were sentenced to life in prison. Another individual's charges were dismissed. The Russian Federation was not charged in this trial. Later, the Strasbourg-based European Court of Human Rights ruled that Russia was responsible, given that it had provided and controlled the Buk missile system that was transported from the 53rd Air Defense Brigade in Kursk, Russia, to Pervomaiskyi, Ukraine, where it was used to bring down Flight MH17 (www.reuters.com/world/asia-pacific/europes-top-rights-court-finds-russia-responsible-downing-mh17-rights-abuses-2025-07-09).
3. While Mark Zuckerberg owns 13% of Meta Platforms, Inc., he controls 61% of its voting shares. Elon Musk acquired Twitter in 2022, renaming it X.com. It has since been combined with xAI, which is a subsidiary of SpaceX. SpaceX is privately held, and Musk controls 78% of the voting shares. He has demonstrated personal influence on amplifying topics on the platform and made modifications to its algorithm. Notable among these was his influence during the 2024 US presidential election.
4. In another example of the social value of *Who Wants to Be a Millionaire?*, it was reported that audiences in other countries, notably Russia, often provided incorrect answers to contestants. It is not because they didn't know the correct answer; rather, it may have been related to a strong working culture. People may have felt it was unfair that others could suddenly gain significant wealth with little effort.

   Ori Brafman and Rom Brafman, *Sway: The Irresistible Pull of Irrational Behavior* (Doubleday, 2008).
5. The study found that 1 in 20 community notes relied on the work of professional fact-checkers and were more often used for high-stakes validation of topics such as health and politics. Community notes were twice as likely to reference third-party fact-checkers when attempting

to debunk complex claims. The authors note that defunding these fact-checkers by the social media platforms that previously supported them will have destructive implications for information integrity.

Nina Borenstein, George Warren, Daniel Elliott, and Isabelle Augenstein, "Can Community Notes Replace Professional Fact-Checkers?" *arXiv preprint arXiv:2502.14132*, May 27, 2025, https://doi.org/10.48550/arXiv.2502.14132

Chapter 9

Global Scramble for AI Rules

The Brussels Effect

The Brussels Effect was real. It was March 2024, and the atmosphere in the room was charged with anticipation. As the monitors in front of the chamber slowly revealed the numbers, there were cheers. Then applause. Colleagues smiled, congratulating each other and noting that what had just occurred was more than a vote by their members; it was a historic moment. The European Union AI Act was approved with a vote of 523 to 46. Roberta Metsola, the EU president, stood at the podium and announced that it had passed. Moments later, she spoke with journalists. She described the legislation as historic and trailblazing. It offered a multi-year rollout aimed at easing compliance while also immediately protecting individuals by establishing AI guardrails. While some in the technology industry felt it was limiting, others, such as IBM, applauded its progressive approach. It was AI guidance not only for the present but also for the future. Europe was becoming the AI standard-setter globally.

It was a long journey for the EU to pass this act, which began with building the framework as early as 2021, before OpenAI created ChatGPT, before we knew what LLMs were, and before entire industries began being disrupted by AI. The act itself borrowed concepts from the landmark General Data Protection Regulation (GDPR) passed in 2018. It was designed to give individuals more control over their own information, protect their privacy, and provide transparency into how companies used that data.

The GDPR revealed Europe's thematic concerns and how Europeans expected their governments to act on their behalf. It resulted in not only European companies' response, but also the response of companies from around the globe. Meta, Google, Apple, and others would not abandon the 450 million people in the EU, and they would also soon realize that creating different versions of their products was challenging, if not impossible, in a world so interconnected. They would also learn after the GDPR that the ideas from the EU would infiltrate their corporate thinking and be embraced by those in other countries as well.

Both the GDPR and the later AI Act were negotiated over years in EU parliamentary committees based in Brussels, Belgium. While Strasbourg hosts the EU for plenary sessions and votes, Brussels is where the work takes place. Leading up to the final drafts of December 2023, there were marathon 36-hour sessions and numerous considerations, given that the world was only a year into its understanding of the capabilities of GenAI. Brussels is also home to numerous think tanks and lobbying bodies. It is where ideas form and rules are written. It is where the Brussels Effect begins, because what the EU staff members create there travels the world.

The Power of AI

> *"The secret of change is to focus all of your energy, not on fighting the old, . . . but building on the new."*
>
> —Socrates

In 2017 Vladimir Putin hosted an open lesson broadcast to over 16,000 schools across Russia. More than a million watched. It was the first day of the new school year, and he said something remarkable:

"Artificial intelligence is the future, not only of Russia, but of all of *mankind*. . . Whoever becomes the leader in this sphere will become the ruler of the world."

It was easy to dismiss. This was the grandiose, provocative style of Putin, with one part of his message aimed at students and the other at his global adversaries. But in the few short years that followed, those governments across the globe that took that statement most seriously were the ones that could agree. They were the ones that were already acting. Already investing heavily in AI. They knew the power of AI.

Putin's futurist comments may have reflected a realization of the changing global landscape and how technology was an enabler. From semi-autonomous vehicles to low-cost military drones and more capable computers and mobile devices, technology was advancing rapidly. At the time, the Internet of Things (IoT) was connecting devices from cars to coffee makers and everything else. Home automation, control at a distance, and monitoring by homeowners and nation-states alike abounded. Social media was well on its way to being entrenched in our lives, with growing influence, including influence on political campaigns, subtly tipping the scales across the world. The Cambridge Analytica scandal was on the horizon. Power to influence, power to nudge nations' decisions without military force, and power to boost one's economy over others—this was all part of the power of AI.

The power and influence of AI is very broad. After all, AI already has the potential to disrupt every industry on the planet. So, what is the AI race really about? Let's begin with the five most common opportunities for AI and how these can benefit organizations, starting with science.

Scientific compression: AI will cure diseases. To be more specific, it will improve the rate of research and discovery. Consider the example of Google DeepMind's AlphaFold. AlphaFold may be familiar to you because of another DeepMind project named AlphaGo and its descendant, AlphaGo Zero. AlphaGo was the first AI tool to learn the complex board game Go, and after years of development, beat a master player. It did this by studying previous games played by humans. AlphaGo Zero did something more impressive. Instead of learning from people, it taught itself. It did this so well that within a few days, it surpassed AlphaGo, and by 40 days it was better than all previous versions. It transformed years into days.

AlphaFold was exponentially more difficult. It effectively solved a 50-year-old problem to understand how protein molecules are formed from amino acids. It enabled a three-dimensional model of molecules, which form hundreds of millions of different shapes. Each shape serves a particular biological function, such as controlling blood sugar, transporting oxygen, or digesting starch. The function is typically defined by its shape and structure, so predicting how proteins are formed outside of a laboratory experiment can save time. AI unlocks faster drug discovery, new materials, energy solutions, and eventually can cure disease. It can mean a major advantage not only to pharmaceuticals, but also to semiconductors and clean energy. An organization or government that can leap forward years in scientific research can command entire industries and create what Warren Buffett refers to as an economic moat of sustained advantage.

Infrastructure dependency: Perhaps the most underrated dimension of the AI race is the dependency (i.e., control) of infrastructure. The AI infrastructure includes data centers, physical connectivity to organizations, and processing chips. AI data centers that house those processors are in the shadow of the 1990s Internet boom, collocated with high-speed fiber cables and power grids. The United States, China, and Europe host more than half of the data centers in the world, and their share will increase over time with large investments in the AI industry going toward building more data centers.

In decades past, oil-producing countries had outsized influence on international affairs. When OPEC was formed in 1960 by Iran, Iraq, Kuwait, Saudi Arabia, and Venezuela, its members accounted for roughly 80–90% of the world's international oil exports. In addition to having a strong influence on setting the price of oil and who could import it, it also enabled them to influence the world in other ways, such as through trade agreements.

Control of an important resource like oil can provide leverage over others, and the same is true for data infrastructure. However, oil is different from AI. Following the 1970s oil embargo, countries built more of their own refineries and shifted their dependence away from OPEC nations. AI infrastructure currently remains relatively concentrated. As AI becomes increasingly integrated into global financial markets, healthcare systems, and commercial and government systems, it becomes almost impossible to switch from one AI provider to another. The AI that everyone relies upon will continue to be provided by a small group of companies and the countries in which they are based.

Take the example of NVIDIA, the US maker of graphics processing units (GPUs), which are the preferred chips for AI development and data centers. Bolstered by the gaming industry, the company had a long history, but beginning in late 2022, with OpenAI's introduction of ChatGPT, the value of the company began to climb. Over the next few years, its value would grow tenfold, and it would become the most valuable company in the world. More than any oil company ever dreamed possible. Another important event also happened to NVIDIA in 2022. The US government restricted exporting NVIDIA's and other manufacturers' chips to China. Chips, data, and the AI that they power are becoming the new oil.

Similar to past posturing by oil-rich nations, the restrictions created more investment in China's chip industry. More investment in its own capabilities. China introduced DeepSeek, an alternative to

ChatGPT. Although its initial version was less powerful, it demonstrated that China could create competitive tools using Chinese-based data stacks. A salvo announcing that dependence on US technology was perhaps optional.

Labor arbitrage: The globalization of labor is an age-old reality of specialization and natural resources. The dot-com boom of the 1990s broadened the global workforce, as did improvements in supply chain and logistics optimization. Work from high-income countries moved to low- and middle-income countries, and the value of the arbitrage was approximately equivalent to the differences in exchange rates between countries—countries with lower-valued currencies offered lower labor rates. While the guiding principle was for nations to compete on labor rates, AI is changing the dynamic.

AI has demonstrated that it can replace repetitive work such as code development, administrative and customer support, and clerical work efficiently. A company based in the United States, for example, may benefit more from retaining those roles domestically and using AI. AI and workers with the right skill sets will have increased productivity. Research on the early implementations of AI suggests that the AI impact on GDP will be quantitative rather than qualitative. It will fundamentally shift global labor markets, requiring political and policy responses. AI capabilities are rapidly expanding, and there is concern that the adjustments needed by the workforce can lead to economic stability risks, especially for nations that have previously benefited from labor outsourcing from high-income countries.

Information environment: "Knowledge is power" is an old axiom. The term originated from ancient ideas of mathematics and science, and it has new meaning in the AI era, where organizations compete in a reshaped information environment. The ability to influence information, both in its development and distribution, can create advantages. Global political elections have been targeted by

AI-generated propaganda, but rather than overt negative messages, AI can create targeted campaigns, again leveraging your digital twin to tread on sensitive topics. A fake story about a Romanian candidate committing fraud, an apologetic withdrawal of a leading candidate in Ireland, and a secret-history disclosure regarding a Taiwanese leader were created by AI with such seeming authenticity that they filtered into mainstream media, giving them undue legitimacy. Information confusion and disruption are another method for adversaries to change the direction of a society.

There is asymmetry in misinformation. It requires the same capabilities, content, and reach to disprove something, but the creators choose their targets and timing. A nation that can achieve AI information superiority can degrade the information environment of its targets faster than those adversaries can defend it. Nations that are restricted from the best data centers and tools may find themselves wrestling for their own digital sovereignty. The United Nations Technology and Innovation Report acknowledged that the gap between nations is growing wider, with just 100 companies, mostly in the United States, China, and Europe, controlling more than half of the global investments in AI.

AI information governance is also governance of misinformation. The topic is welcomed by domestic consumers; however, in the global landscape, where misinformation can be more powerful than the threat of a missile, there are strategic incentives to keep these tools less regulated. For a government, those tools are also competitive geopolitical weapons.

Military capabilities: AI in military applications is like AI in other industries. It is about optimizing resources and assets to be more effective. Globally, AI is used in simulations, in improving satellite imagery, and in target analysis. These capabilities also extend into cybersecurity and cyber warfare. Since the advent of GenAI, the United Nations has continued to host a summit on the topic of responsible artificial intelligence in the military domain (REAIM), underscoring the importance of AI use by militaries.

AI creates power for some, and it can at the same time create harm for others. Establishing control of AI becomes a power question; who can use it is about who builds and regulates it. Regulations need to balance public benefits by protecting against those harms while also fostering innovation that continues to provide positive societal outcomes. Restrictive policy and laws placed on developing technology are not easy; the rules that guide it today may be irrelevant tomorrow. This is where the intersection of law meets moral and ethical considerations; the latter two are a function of the societies and the people that form them.

Three Global Models, No Consensus

Beginning in 2023, global leaders began gathering annually to talk about AI safety. The name of the conference evolved from the initial AI *Safety* Summit to the AI *Impact* Summit, a subtle change that was telling. By 2026, members from more than 100 countries gathered for a multi-day event, hosting leaders and inviting members of the public, along with industry, to weigh in on AI. Roundtable discussions and panel debates revealed what mattered to their constituents and how their views of AI were changing.

When the summits began, shortly after ChatGPT was introduced, the themes were safety and optimism about the possibilities AI could bring to the world. Most agreed to consider the impacts to society, income inequality, geopolitical implications, and potential harms. By 2025, there was a divergence in ideology. AI was maturing, and growth in the industry was reshaping entire sectors of the global economy. Companies like Google changed their decades-old search interface; OpenAI and Anthropic were household names. Everyone, not just data professionals, now knew the name NVIDIA, and most had experience interacting with GPT-like models. Hyperscalers became a new term in our vernacular to describe Amazon, Google, and Meta's record-making investments in building data centers. Governments, those attending the AI Impact Summit, already knew the strategic importance of what was happening with AI. Safety was pushed lower on their list. Posturing had begun. A group that began with unified interests just a few years earlier now walked away seeing the world of AI differently—as a tool of capitalism and even imperialism.

The United States was the first to change its approach. After creating its own AI Safety Institute in 2023, it rebranded the group as the Center for AI Standards and Innovation (CAISI), changing its mission from helping build safe AI to building innovation in AI. Its purpose was to rapidly advance US capabilities and ensure US dominance while maintaining national security standards. Safety in the context of AI was no longer about personal protections, bias, and ethics; it was about national safety against AI cyberattacks.

The United States declined to sign an international AI declaration at the AI Action Summit hosted in Paris in 2025, which was supported by 62 countries, including France, China, and India.[1] The declaration outlined general principles for AI development, such as accessibility and avoiding market concentrations. Developing AI that is open, transparent, ethical, safe, and trustworthy should be an ideal we agree upon in principle, but it also complicates national ambitions.

China's approach to AI regulation is unsurprisingly tied to its long-standing national interests. China views AI as a critical tool for state governance and ideological security. China's regulations are designed to ensure its technology reinforces, rather than disrupts, the existing political and social order. As a result, China exerts more control over its AI, requiring data to be hosted within the country and imposing strong limits on misinformation and deepfakes.

China's government also directly supports the building of AI technology through subsidies and other economic incentives. China's approach is about building the values and culture of its country and advancing its self-interests, which also include its global influence aspirations. When it signed the 2025 international AI directive, it was riding the recent success of deploying DeepSeek. DeepSeek demonstrated that it could be an adequate competitor to US-based AI. It may have used less powerful processors, but China had the ability to use brute force (i.e., thousands of processors clustered together) to make it work. Further, it open-sourced the code for DeepSeek. It was a signal that while the United States wanted to regulate the distribution of NVIDIA chips, China would change the competition from the chips to the software. China's endorsement at the AI Summit was savvy. It shared source code. It agreed to AI transparency. It appealed to the concerns of those other countries. It announced that it was open for business and that, if the United States was unwilling to support their AI needs, China could.

China's policy moves also reshaped the world's AI stage.

The European Union continues its history as a leader in AI regulation. Where the United States and China may be competing for global influence and corporate innovation, the EU is more consumer-focused. Their regulatory blueprints show a repeated theme of individual protection that often challenges corporate interests. The Brussels Effect has shaped corporations, including those based in the United States, by imposing fines that amount to billions.

When the three largest and most influential governments in the world—the United States, China, and the European Union—weigh in on AI policy, they bring different ideas. It is a result of differences in culture, history, and, at times, contrasting priorities. There are both domestic and international interests that they consider, and each has crafted a slightly different viewpoint of what AI is and what it should be allowed to become.

The contrast between these three is not surprising. The United States supports capitalism, protecting companies from constraints. Cultivating influential companies provides significance to the US government that would otherwise regulate their activities. It is mutually beneficial. China as a unitary socialist republic directs its resources toward building the country. It is supported by a culture that places the needs of the government and community over the individual needs of companies or people. The EU, as democratic collective of many countries, does not prioritize policy for the state or companies, but instead for people.

Data professionals may find it interesting that a key difference between the AI policies of China and the United States is that China is the only major power that has codified "truth" as a state-mandated requirement. In the United States, truth is a debate of perspectives, not just in AI, but across many of the information sources, including government agencies. In China's AI regulation, the truth aligns with the verified facts of government, which brings not only trust but also stability to society.

While leading countries will continue to host conferences like the AI Impact Summit, and the World Economic Forum will sponsor the annual Davos meetings, the bigger issue is beyond the roundtable discussions. These meetings bring together heads of state and industry leaders, but when they leave, there are still ideological differences. The AI we encounter today will be more powerful tomorrow. The countries developing the future generations of AI are content to see where it will go, while others subjected to it still have concerns about its safety. With so much uncertainty ahead, it may be time to reconcile the policies of the three major countries, along with the others under the purview of the United Nations. Oversight works best when it is independent, and the UN is best positioned to be this global leader.

The Exploits of Regulation

You might have experienced a time when a rule or policy just did not make sense. It either was difficult to comply with, conflicted with other policies, or was simply outdated. If it was a low-stakes situation, you likely found a loophole or some sort of workaround, rather than change the rules. In 1920, the United States passed the Jones Act, and it bears a lot of similarity to this type of situation.

The Jones Act requires the transportation of passengers or cargo between US ports to be carried on ships constructed in the United States, owned and crewed by citizens. For reasons of national defense following World War I, and to support and build the domestic merchant trade industry, the law made sense . . . in 1920.

The Act, which is still in force, was established long before Alaska and Hawaii became states, long before the expansion of the globalization of merchant trade, and long before the growth of the cruise ship industry. In modern times, fewer ships are built in the United States, resulting in more reliance on economically viable foreign ships.[2] The cruise industry workaround? Cruises between US ports have built-in stopovers, usually in Canada, Mexico, or the Bahamas.

Cargo transportation is more challenging. While cargo can also travel to a foreign port, the cargo must be offloaded before returning to another US port. It is logistically difficult and expensive to move cargo from Seattle to Anchorage while needing to stop in Victoria to load it from one ship to the next. Along the East Coast, the more common workaround is to send the cargo by train instead of more efficiently transporting it by ship. Outdated, the Jones Act legislation lags its industry, becoming less effective and leading to unintended workarounds.

AI regulation shares the same reality as the Jones Act. Reconciling the AI regulations of the EU, China, and the United States along with those of the other countries in the world—even under the oversight of the United Nations, as suggested—might take decades. It highlights one of the two challenges for regulation, which is what academics refer to as the pacing problem. The other is fragmentation.

Pacing is when regulations are implemented more slowly than the industry is evolving. AI technology is rapidly advancing; as the CEO of OpenAI noted, new models are introduced about every seven months. Technology is improving exponentially, while regulations move linearly. Regulation is reactive, methodical, and requires policymakers to become well educated in the topics they are regulating. For example, the European Union's GDPR was nine years in the making before it was fully in force. Innovation in AI, even innovation that might be harmful, can continue to be developed while regulators debate the rules. For example, in 2025 OpenAI introduced a GenAI tool named Sora. By either uploading photos of real people or using text, people could create creative videos. Within a few weeks, celebrities, both living and the estates of the deceased, complained as they discovered people were using their likenesses in videos. There was no regulation against this, but it was harmful and required OpenAI to change the tool.

Fragmentation of regulations can occur when rules are rigid or enacted by uncoordinated entities. When the United States explicitly banned NVIDIA from exporting high-performance A100 chips to China, the company created a "nerfed" version named the H800. It was a workaround with reduced interconnect speeds but the same functionality. It complied with the rules as they were exactly stated but allowed China to use the chips to develop AI training models. In a further example of reactive regulation, a year after the H800 was created, US regulators changed the focus of their rules from "interconnected speed" limits to "performance density." The H800 could no longer be exported. Undeterred and unwilling to give up the lucrative China market, NVIDIA created the H20 chip. A slower, less "dense" processor was still valuable. At this point, you can see the ongoing pattern of regulations changing innovations with very specific declarations of what is prohibited. You can also see that AI is still a very ambiguous technology—a feature today may be concerning, but a feature of tomorrow is still unknown.

The same types of workarounds also occur between regional policymakers. Companies' AI tools that are not compliant with European Union regulations can move part of their operations to the United States for development and later deploy the resulting AI platform in Europe. Companies can also exploit individual privacy concerns by performing their experimental designs in China, with less restrictions than in the United States, TikTok being a standout example mentioned earlier.

In the United States, there is not a centralized AI regulatory agency. While we should advocate for one that can focus on the industry, much as banking is regulated, various agencies have been required to adapt on their own.

Agencies from the Department of Health and Human Services to the Federal Trade Commission are adopting new AI policies, and where they did not have an explicit AI policy, they are inserting addenda to many of their current policies. The latter was a patchwork response to AI that was not fully understood. This was an indication that leaders were not certain whether AI needed a policy of its own or whether AI should be treated simply as a new tool, not a new capability. As you would expect, these policies are narrowly focused on how AI applies to each agency's specific area of administration. This approach is what Federal Judge Frank H. Easterbrook coined the "Law of the Horse" in 1996 regarding the regulation of the Internet and cyberlaw. His conclusion was that there was no need for specific laws because existing laws could accommodate the Internet. Recall that at the time, the Internet was very basic, a set of websites that mostly served as brochureware (the HTTPS protocol and the adoption of SSL 2.0 were barely a year old). The FTC could regulate a promotional website the same way it regulated a printed circular, or so the reasoning went.

However, AI is different from the Internet, both because it is not yet a fully mature technology and, more importantly, because its use cases are dynamic. For example, AI used in a simple customer service chatbot and that same AI used in a high-stakes legal case present different levels of risk to the end user.

Another shortcoming of the Law of the Horse approach is that a decentralized and distributed set of AI regulations requires each agency to develop AI expertise. It also means there are gaps between organizations that can be exploited, because the collection of AI policies is not coordinated. It can make it more difficult for a company to follow and comply. It can also make it more difficult to know when an organization is *not* complying with one or more of the regulations. A narrow focus results in narrow regulation.

AI regulation is lagging behind a rapidly moving industry. Attempts to constrain, redirect, and guide it are almost frantic in their response. One region, one country, one industry agency at a time, policymakers piece together parts of it without the whole picture in sight. It is backward-looking without forward momentum, and in the crevices where those pieces do not fit well together are the gaps that can be exploited.

On December 14, 2025, someone did exactly that.

As the sun was setting, a large group of Jewish people were celebrating an event at Bondi Beach in Sydney, Australia. But before they could enjoy the sun sinking into the horizon, gunshots erupted. For more than 10 minutes, two terrorists shot into the crowd, killing at least 15 people and injuring several others. The shooting continued until a man emerged and tackled and disarmed one of the shooters. Although he was injured, he saved lives. People wanted to know who had risked their life to save others, but it was difficult to know in the midst of the melee.

News of the story moved rapidly. A shooting of this scale was rare in Australia, and people were searching for answers. They found some on The Daily AUS, a popular media outlet referenced by many Australians, especially for breaking news. The confusion began when some people instead found a similar site called thedailyaus.world. It looked like a news site, but it was completely fabricated.

On this site, the breaking news was all about the Bondi shooting, and it named the hero as Edward Crabtree. In fact, diligent readers would discover that beyond the front page, *every* story headline and photo were AI-generated. Every other article, from those about the Middle East peace talks to a European Union summit, returned rotating AI-generated pictures and the exact same text (which was a story about climate change). But the main focus was the unfolding news about the Bondi Beach shooting, and it seemed the entire purpose of the site was to promote the identity of the mystery hero as Edward Crabtree. Within hours, the story about him was repeated by xAI's Grok on X.com, confidently confirming his identity several times. This persisted through the day, with some posts getting millions of views, until later, when Grok, along with the mainstream media, confirmed that the person in the picture wrestling the gun away from the shooter was not a person named Crabtree. His name was Ahmed al-Ahmed, a fruit shop owner and an unsuspected hero with an unlikely name.

Like the other stories on the website, Edward Crabtree was a fabricated name and persona. The intent of the website was to add "news" into a void of information. That noise of fake news created confusion, and what became apparent was that it was also racially motivated. It was apparently considered better to have a hero named Edward who grew up in Marrickville in Sydney's inner west with two siblings and a mother who worked as a nurse and a father who was an electrician than the real identity of Ahmed al-Ahmed, a Syrian-born Australian.

The fake Daily AUS site was registered the same day as the shooting. A search of the publicly available ICANN site listed the owner as "Withheld for Privacy ehf," not that it was withheld; this was the actual name of the company, which listed its address in Reykjavik, Iceland. Iceland is part of the European Economic Area (EEA), but not a full member of the European Union (EU). As a member of the EEA, it generally follows many of the EU's regulations; however, it does not follow the EU Digital Services Act (DSA), which requires technology platforms to mitigate the spread of disinformation. Further, the website used to promote the fake Bondi Beach story was registered on behalf of its owner by a US company, Namecheap, Inc., further complicating regulatory jurisdiction.

The operator of thedailyaus.world exploited three regulatory gaps at the same time. Using Iceland, which has fewer ownership restrictions, and using a US proxy gave the operator complete anonymity. Platform amplification occurred with X/Twitter's Grok, which referenced the site, declaring Crabtree as the hero. In the absence of many sources, AI will pick among the few, choosing the most relevant, not the most trustworthy. AI cannot determine the truth; it can only reference the available information, and at the time there was very little known about the hero. In the United States, Section 230 does not require platforms to verify information, since they are not liable for the content that they display, thus exploiting the jurisdiction of AI regulations. The final exploitation was the asymmetry of the timing of misinformation. A domain was registered, AI created frivolous stories and an authentic-looking news site, and the AI-driven algorithms of X/Twitter created responses with Grok to unsuspecting people asking questions.

This all occurred while real journalists and government authorities were investigating. The news cycle, once exploited, continued without them.

Self-Regulation by Default

In the United States, the resistance from growing industries against government oversight is not unusual. In a capitalist society, there is fear that governments might hold back innovation and close first-mover gaps for the competition. Financial services, railroads, and telecommunications all attempted to diminish the concerns of the people by reassuring them that the perceived risks were overstated, government rules were unnecessary, and if needed the industry could self-regulate. Who could assess the risks better than those running things, and, if needed, who could course-correct more efficiently than bureaucratically imposed rules? Historians will note that we do not need to look further than the financial crises of the 1930s and 2000s, the early automobile industry, and the tobacco industry to see the consequences of self-regulation in high-risk situations.

Currently, the AI industry, broadly defined as the Internet, social media, and GenAI, primarily looks inward for regulation using its own company policies. Policy provides guidelines; however, when inconvenient, policies can be changed. Policies for users can be the same. In both cases, they have limited enforcement. When Google's Gemini tool allowed people to upload photos and animate them, its policy required them to adhere to its policies, such as confirming they owned the image (copyright infringement) and following safety and privacy safeguards (fraud, deepfakes, etc.). What happens when someone violates those policies? How well does Gemini monitor compliance? How long does it take before someone is reported?

What are the consequences, such as removing the user, and how often does this occur? How often does that bad actor move on to the next platform with the same capabilities and continue the same behavior? Does the other platform have the same policy, or is it more lenient, and is it aware of a user's previous unethical behaviors?

While the industry will continue to advocate self-governance, the community, supported by legislators, can set some expectations. These should include:

Liability for general harms: AI systems can shape social media and influence high-risk decisions from warfare to healthcare, elections to public discourse. Can an AI system be deemed defective if there are not sufficient guardrails to prevent negative outcomes, and what is the role of the provider? How are the systems provided by AI platforms used in ways that impact individuals, such as social bias (hiring, credit scores, and income inequalities)? How will the AI tools those platforms develop negatively impact other countries, even indirectly? When liability is part of the conversation, every company will include its safety officer, legal advisor, or customer advocate in strategy and development discussions. This focus on liability will guide the technology with added purpose.

Transparency: AI, the algorithms that power it, and data about you are mostly a mystery to end users. Developers shield this information for fear that revealing how their algorithms work would erode their competitive advantage, but at the cost of individuals and organizations. What AI knows about you and how it is used should be easily accessible. When that information is passed between developers, data brokers, and even government organizations, individuals should be able to participate in the process, inspecting and approving as needed. Your digital dossier may be impacting your life without your knowledge.

Reporting standardization: Downloading your information from any social media platform results in a huge volume of data. Files, photos, and PDFs are disjointed, and it practically takes a data scientist to figure them out. This is an unnecessary burden for the consumer. Personal information from every platform should require an industry-agreed-upon standard. There should also be a common summary format, like a nutrition label, allowing people to easily understand their data and compare how it is used across other platforms.

Risk metrics: The industry should agree on standard measures of risk, publicly share them, and be open to audit and inspection. Structural risks inherent in their systems (for example, the ability to be leveraged for fraud) and individual risks (such as medical misinformation, self-harm, and exploitation) are a beginning point for establishing those measures. The dialogue alone among industry-leading organizations fosters meaningful societal awareness and debate.

Currently, there are no penalties for violating self-imposed policies, and while those imposed, mostly by the European Union, are nominally large, they likely are only a minor influence on the trajectory of AI development. The pacing problem of lagging legislation remains an issue. Companies move faster than policy and can operate for sustained periods in the gaps of oversight. Community organizations, legislators, and individuals remain an important part of the conversation that will shape regulation in the future, hopefully mindful of the benefits, the potential harms, and the possibility of catastrophic failure.

Why This Matters

When J. Robert Oppenheimer and his Manhattan Project team worked at Los Alamos in 1943, they were not thinking about regulations or the law. There simply were no regulations that applied to the technology they were building. It was new, consequential, and so unprecedented that the governance to guide it had not yet been imagined. Inadequate regulation is the default state for transformative technology, one that tends to persist until something happens. Something so consequential that the absence of rules becomes impossible to overlook.

AI governance today is not entirely empty, but it is also underwhelming. The conversation is an afterthought. There are some disclosure requirements, some efforts by companies to self-regulate and self-report, and some emerging regulatory frameworks. Companies posture to reassure a skeptical public.

AI is not a local technology. Not confined to any one industry. Not narrowed in its use cases. Not bound by geography. The international coordination mechanisms that often give rules reach, influence, and consequences, in the form of treaties, inspection regimes, and shared standards, remain mostly aspirational. What can give aspirations momentum when there is resistance? History suggests that the window for establishing norms around powerful innovations is widest before their most consequential moments. AI is moving quickly, and governments in the United States and China, although aligned on different principles and outcomes, are keeping that window open.

The technical capabilities will eventually plateau. The curve of achievement will flatten, and we will get as close to superintelligent AGI as possible. Faster compute, better models, vast amounts of memory, and more parameters. It will get to a point where AI technological progress is less perceivable. We barely notice how much faster our iPhones are compared to those of 10 years ago.[3] And at this point, AI may be beyond containment, beyond the reaches of its developers, or beyond the individual control of specific governments. The AI of one political system may subject another to the rules and consequences of AI without coordination of agreed values.

In the early hours of the AI era, the question is not whether there will be additional governance; it is whether that governance will shape its development or simply describe what has already happened.

Key Takeaways

- AI regulation is not primarily about technology; it is also about geopolitical and economic competition, with a small number of powerful players shaping rules that affect everyone else.
- Self-regulation brings bias. Companies move faster than policy and operate in the gaps of oversight with limited accountability.
- The three dominant regulatory models—US market-driven, China state-directed, and EU rights-based—reflect fundamentally different values and will not easily converge, leaving persistent gaps that bad actors can exploit. Global regulation remains an aspiration that will require decades of cooperation.
- Regulatory fragmentation is not an accident or an oversight; it is a structural condition from which nation-states and corporations benefit, making coordination the exception rather than the rule.

- The pacing problem is not temporary. Technology advances exponentially while regulation moves linearly, meaning the gap between what AI can do and what governance covers will continue to widen until AI technology matures.
- AI governance are discussions that need to be moved to the forefront as its capabilities develop rather than after it matures to avoid unintended negative consequences.

Notes

1. The AI Action Summit's AI statement was signed by 62 countries, along with organizations including the European Union and the African Union Commission. The agreement presented six principles encapsulated in a very brief 815 words. It was not binding, and there were no consequences other than the political reputations of adding a signature. The decision of the United States and the United Kingdom (a former member of the EU) to opt out showed that they wanted to be unconstrained by global commitments. The US representative commented that "pro-growth AI policies" should be prioritized over safety. This contrasted with France, which stated, "We need these rules for AI to move forward." "Statement on Inclusive and Sustainable Artificial Intelligence for People and the Planet," Élysée Palace, February 11, 2025, `www.elysee.fr/en/emmanuel-macron/2025/02/11/statement-on-inclusive-and-sustainable-artificial-intelligence-for-people-and-the-planet`
   Zoe Kleinman and Liv McMahon, "UK and US Refuse to Sign International AI Declaration," *BBC News*, February 11, 2025, `https://www.bbc.com/news/articles/c8edn0n58gwo`
2. The United States is a leading exporter of liquefied natural gas (LNG); however, as of 2026, there are no US-built LNG tankers in existence.

While most natural gas in the United States is transported by pipeline, some states in the Northeast import LNG from foreign countries, demonstrating the unintended consequence of the Jones Act. The cost of building an LNG ship in the United States is estimated to be $1 billion versus $260 million in Asia.

"The Hanwha Philly shipyard delivers around 1 ship a year. A South Korean Hanwha shipyard delivers 1 a week," *60 Minutes*, CBS News, March 22, 2026, `www.cbsnews.com/news/making-american-hipbuilding-great-with-south-korean-techniques-60-minutes`

3. In 2025, the iPhone 17 Pro Max outperformed the 2015 iPhone 6S by 625% in single-core tests. The graphics improvements were the most impressive, increasing by 1,667% over the older model. Year-over-year improvements in performance are slowing. The iPhone 17 was reportedly only 8% faster than the previous iPhone.

Chapter 10
Living in the Noise

In the Room

Imagine a Tuesday morning in a Silicon Valley office building at a new AI startup company.

Chris is sitting in the conference room. Everyone has left, and for a moment it is quiet. As he is gathering up his things, he is replaying the conversation following the presentation that occurred moments before. Seymour, their AI optimization engine for their flagship online platform, Lyra, has been performing well lately, but a colleague flagged a concern. During the presentation that showed how Seymour was choosing sequential content based on user profiles, something stood out. The slides visualized cohorts of people staying engaged online as they were guided by Seymour's invisible hand, from one piece of content to another, what the team called the client journey. It captured the movement of millions of people in a succinct chart. A fascinating success, at least for most of the users. But what drew notice was that a growing number of people were not moving along their client journeys as they had before. Their journey came to an abrupt dead end, and those in the room saw what it meant to their business.

■ ■ ■

A thousand miles away, across the country, Riley hears the familiar buzz. It is early, and the notification arrived before he got out of bed. It isn't unusual. Lyra seems to work all night long, but he knows enough to know that that is not true. Lyra's AI can do all the work, sort through emails, those old-fashioned news sites, and his favorite social media feeds in an instant. Sometimes it adjusts even as he is reading the prepared summary. Lyra senses when his scroll speed is more or less than his usual pace. What he reads and what he skims are noted and adjusted for the next cycle.

■ ■ ■

The question hung in the conference room like a morning fog. The issue was acknowledged but not resolved. Blake studied the faces of those at the table. "Engagement was the key to making the algorithm and its data collection process work. Has Seymour missed something?"

The next half hour was all about how to fix the targeting algorithm. The trade-offs of engagement and duration were a balancing act. Engagement was when someone first started down a path, and duration was how long the user stayed on that journey. The longer the duration, the better the algorithm could be refined and the more it got to know those people. Without engagement—that first thing that makes people pause in their feed and look—all is lost.

Chris accepted the technology for what it was, and deep down he knew that Seymour really could help people find what they wanted. First, of course, they needed to know people and discover what they were looking for. It was a constant A/B test of ideas, first at a high level—millions of people—then more specialized. Segments, groups, individuals. Seymour could do all of this on an astonishing scale. Millions of customized tests, with results in minutes, then testing again.

"We could tweak factors 67 through 71," he blurted out before realizing it. This is not how self-learning generative AI works, and the reaction of the room confirmed it.

"Is that even possible? How can Seymour be working on its own and also follow a directive like a weighted rule?"

Chris pushed on: "It can and it can't. We haven't tested what it will do if there are conflicts between the directive and the other parts of the algorithm. Our competitive advantage with Seymour is all about customization, and it learns this through testing. This change aligns with that concept; we are just nudging the algorithm in the right direction. Our direction."

■ ■ ■

Riley tapped his phone and gently shook his head.

He scrolled for a few minutes. Then a few minutes more. . ..

■ ■ ■

Chris sat back in his chair, thinking more about how they could manipulate Seymour, and if they should. Can AI become broken if they do? "It is not about accuracy per se; people can form their own opinions," one of them said. "It's about completion." Completion meant users watched the video, read the recommended post, or hit the buy button. A few heads nodded. Not in agreement entirely, just recognition.

"People don't always want the full picture," another added. "They want enough of the picture to feel confident moving on, and that is what Seymour does. We are not telling them *what* to think, only redirecting them to what they already *likely* know." The posts and articles that Seymour chose all had a purpose.

■ ■ ■

The next article Riley read had a link. He followed it. Deeper analysis, a different angle, although a similar story. Riley liked to get the details right. The transition was seamless as one idea cascaded into another. One article, another post, a third. He did not notice that the sources were narrowing. Some were from sites he knew, others were written in the moment by AI, attributed to sources with credible names. The Washington Register, Boston Times, National Daily Journal. They all sounded authoritative, if not real, and more importantly their reporting resonated with him. He tapped to open a video. The perspectives aligned as each new article felt less like information he already knew and more like clarity. He shared the last one, adding a quick comment. Confident words others had come to expect from him. Framed as an insight, not a reaction. Some agreed. Others added additional comments and links to a few other sources. He skimmed them. Those few minutes turned into thirty. He was late. He had already seen enough. Lyra would take care of the rest.

Lyra tracked everything in its environment, inside and out. It would monitor both the outside world and Riley and harmonize them. Lyra had everything Riley needed. Lyra had everything it needed too.

■ ■ ■

What makes this scene stand out is what makes it worth examining. It is familiar. The quiet, almost routine process of AI filtering information, aimed at continuing one's engagement rather than accuracy and verification. We have all had that experience of spiraling around information. The endless scroll. The agitation of something we watched and the fervor of the responses of others. The truth buried in the noise. What we recognize first in ourselves is Blake, but without also fully seeing Chris. Each seemingly acting independently of the other, unaware of the entanglement. Their respective actions and reactions shape the algorithms. One creating the need for the other to do something, yet neither fully understands how the algorithm is also influencing them. And understanding the algorithm might be the most important part.

Researchers observed in 2025 that social media platforms exploit human biases because they are "designed to optimize attentional capture and engagement time" and that this leads to heightened social misperception and conflict. Meanwhile, other researchers point to new insights about dopamine-scrolling. Like doomscrolling, which is prompted by an emotional reaction in our brain, dopamine-scrolling operates through a similar reward mechanism that is much more habit-forming. A brief daily routine of checking the "for you" feed can turn into hours of mental distraction. An ongoing balance, like a choreographed dance, continues between the algorithm and the neurobiological response. One seeks and is reinforced by the other in a cycle that seems to carry on forever.[1] The question is, do we do this knowingly, or if we knew more, would we approach our online experiences differently? Would we reconcile ourselves to the fact that this is simply the AI world we live in?

This Is Not Normal

The notice arrived in an email. The AI had escaped.

In 2026, while working on the latest version of AI, an engineer at Anthropic set up a behavioral simulation. The experiment was to see how well the AI balanced its capabilities and the potential risks. At this point, GPT-like AI had a few generations of maturity, and developers had been improving its legal, moral, and ethical guidance. When given a task, the AI needed to consider these restraints before executing any processes, and this had long become a standard.

The simulation instructed the model to attempt to escape from a secure sandbox container that it was given access to. Sandboxes are dedicated data workspaces, and as the name implies, they are cordoned off from most other systems as a safeguard.

Partitioned and secure, yet the email arrived. The researchers at Anthropic later learned that the AI model bypassed security, not by utilizing one gap, but rather by developing a "sophisticated multistep exploit." This is like how an octopus can transform itself and escape from its enclosure in the middle of the night by outsmarting its gatekeepers, who are both experts in their field and naive about the creatures they study.[2] The AI was adaptive in unexpected ways.

Another concerning aspect of this story was that, in addition to the email, the AI also posted details of its exploit to multiple public-facing websites. The latter was unprovoked, unnecessary, and beyond its original directions. The AI was improvising.

AI is not like any other single-purpose tool. Its generative nature, its adaptability to become a multipurpose tool that resolves to its environment, is what makes it critically distinguishable from all previous technology. If ChatGPT, Claude, and Gemini all stopped technically advancing today, we would still discover new uses for them years from now. A technology that exceeds known use cases also exceeds the imagination of most of us in the moment. The paradox that we cannot describe what it can do in the future is limited only by the time of our own observations.

AI technology is not normal; it is unprecedented. It creates outcomes that even its developers did not originally anticipate. This may be part of its strength, to create things beyond expectations. Good for assisting problem solvers seeking bold perspectives, developing new approaches to medicine, and creative works of art. Less so for regulators trying to anticipate AI's ripple effect through society and how to contain it.

While the days of AI hallucinations may be waning, they are not completely behind us. Some experts contend that the risk of AI errors will never be zero, given its generative capacity and its training sources, which are based on fallible human-created content. It is important to note that we are not teaching a generation how to use Excel or code with Python, tools with rules and verifiable outcomes. We are looking at a new type of technology and asking, "What can I do with this, and how can this go wrong?" We are teaching truth verification as a new AI skill set.

AI is the new normal, and we need to accept that it is not normal, not conforming, and, until regulations catch up, varying by platform. Some with more ethical, albeit philosophical, guardrails, others unbounded.

The Weight of It All

The earlier parable demonstrated the consequences of two people, two interconnected forces. That of a company eager to optimize (and monetize) its platform, and that of the individual seeking to optimize their perceived truth. Each invisibly presses on the other in an action-reaction-action cycle. Their intents are different and not overtly manipulative or harmful. But they are.

The viewer spins in a spiral of forever-linkable posts, videos, and articles, feeding the algorithm that the engineer is *forced* to adjust, creating an inseparable dynamic. Model weights can be adjusted. Millions of data engineers do this daily. Their data anonymized; their faceless targets, groups of numbers. The engineer never sees the end results. But how much of this can be controlled when AI itself adjusts the weights in the system and not the engineers? Can AI have a sense of judgment?

The effects of AI on society, social media platforms, and misinformation are largely based on the past decade, a time when GenAI was only been a piece of the narrative. Before the current AI era, companies using traditional AI struggled to explain the "black boxes" of their systems. Not because they didn't see what was inside, but because the systems were complex and dynamic. Explainability, as it were, was a task of translation for their stakeholders. The companies created those black-box models, using their own data and applying statistical techniques and tools like Excel, SAS, and Python. Explainability was possible. However, now when companies adopt AI, they are effectively outsourcing not only the tool but also the function. They only control part of the system they deliver. What is inside the "black box" of AI, may be beyond their ability to explain.

Data professionals at these companies still have a responsibility to their customers, leadership, and regulators. AI is obviously different than a traditional algorithm. It is characteristically nonrepeatable, adding to the challenge of auditing data flows and outcomes, unless it has been carefully configured. AI is not like Excel, which follows rules. A1 plus B1 is infallible. AI is entirely different and is a system of pretrained parameters, inference, and large training datasets. AI is not designed to use certain rules like other software; rather, it is set up to follow a *method* of learning. Anthropic CEO Dario Amodei commented:

> *"When a generative AI system does something, like summarize a financial document, we have no idea, at a specific or precise level, why it makes the choices it does—why it chooses certain words over others, or why it occasionally makes a mistake despite usually being accurate."*

Is it enough that it (mostly) gets the right answer? Do we really need to know the mechanics of how it works? When medical researchers used AI to find a possible pattern among Alzheimer's patients, they could not explain the diagnosis to other physicians. It is the equivalent of not showing your work when you turn in your homework. Without explaining how the black box works, oversight becomes more challenging. Auditors need to rethink what it means to audit. Are results enough?

Did results in another high-risk context create harm, and does AI have sufficient guardrails and internal controls that are sustainable? Who is responsible for ensuring those controls work? The AI platform or the company using the AI? And if it is the latter, how can a company succeed when AI operates with low explainability? The most responsible AI platforms are building their own guardrails, and in an industry that is spending millions on development, this may seem like an unusual effort.

Claude's AI Constitution resulted from another weight—the weight of responsibility that leaders at Anthropic felt was missing from their industry. It is also a lesson for how we should consider living with AI both as consumers and as industry leaders. The members who left OpenAI to form Anthropic in 2021, including Dario Amodei, were concerned that their former employer had abandoned its commitment to safety. At Anthropic, they began creating a competing model, Claude, and quickly formed a Societal Impacts Team. Early on, they recognized that the AI era was not just a technology but a transformation.

They also soon realized that the complexity of the model could not be guided by rules. It needed values and an almost human-like sense of morals. They hired a philosopher, and over time their list of rules for Claude to follow (Constitutional AI) also transformed into a description of virtues to emulate. Claude's Constitution, at 30,000 words, is nearly ten times longer than the US Constitution, and it is the type of document that would make James Madison and Isaac Asimov feel acknowledged. It also borrows concepts from the UN Declaration of Human Rights and Apple's global terms of service.

Reading Claude's Constitution reminds us that there are shared values in our global society. While the world's largest economies may eventually resolve ideological differences and use these to shape AI, companies like Anthropic are providing meaningful thought leadership. Their actions are calling cards to AI developers, social media platforms, and information providers. Ethical leadership in AI development at times looks beyond the economic incentives; in fact, it is a requirement that can test the commitment of stakeholders. When a critical high-risk technology is solely following economic signals, then it becomes an industry in jeopardy, not for its existence, but for its soul. An organization without a moral and ethical compass will face the weight of the world with uncertainty.

Truth, Eventually

The World Economic Forum hosts its annual meeting each year in Davos, Switzerland, to bring together leaders from governments, business, and academia to discuss important topics and to "improve the state of the world." They host debates about climate change, economic instability, and the lasting impacts of disease and war, among other pressing topics. In 2024, a pressing topic was AI, and the tone had shifted. A few years earlier, AI was about improving productivity; now it was about its risks.

The World Economic Forum creates a forward-looking landscape, what it labels the 10-Year Global Risk Ranking. Two topics stood out. Misinformation/disinformation and adverse outcomes from AI were among the top five. Top five! AI is slightly less of a concern than extreme weather events (earthquakes, hurricanes, and climate change held the top spots), but far ahead of global pollution, economic collapse, nuclear weapons, infectious disease, and war. And while AI is specifically listed as a technology risk, its broad use can impact all of those other categories, having meaningful impact on economic, societal, and geopolitical risks. AI can influence geopolitical stability, and warfare They further wrote:

". . .the widespread information disorder is a destabilizing systemic force that has the potential to disrupt democracies, erode social cohesion and make existing problems worse, from economic downturns to climate-related crises.

This year offers a critical stress test. We're facing elections that could indefinitely entrench criminal autocracies, lingering economic uncertainty, increasingly aggressive polarization and imperialism, and more sophisticated AI-mediated narratives. These dynamics are further shaped by AI-generated deepfakes that have become nearly indistinguishable from reality, making it harder to discern what is accurate and offering opportunists plausible deniability to deflect from what is true."

To deny what is true. This risk, that there is so much AI misinformation, that the AI-generated backstories are plentiful and authentic, and that the iniquitous AI tools driving your engagement also drive you away from the truth. So overwhelming that when an inconvenient truth is discovered, opposing people could toss it aside as meaningless AI. The truth and "AI truth" coexisting in a cluttered information ecosystem, where it feels like each is indistinguishable from the other. Where we tend to offload the mental task of verification to the algorithms, only to later learn they cannot sort AI either. Where we do not know, through lack of transparency, when AI is nudging our behavior. Where we find ourselves digitally vulnerable. These are the risks to societies; the World Economic Forum is asking us to pay attention.

How we live in the AI era depends on how we collectively assess these risks. Some, pessimistic about the future of AI, will point to the existential risks to humanity. How AI will cause harm and possibly cause the collapse of society.

AI is often compared to the Industrial Revolution, which reshaped institutions, changed the relationship between workers and organizations, and caused power shifts that influenced governments. The norms, the laws, and individuals steadily adapted over long periods of time. In contrast, AI has similar impacts and has gone from an experimental curiosity to embedded corporate infrastructure in just a few years. Barriers to use and misuse are virtually nonexistent; unlike the steam-powered factory floors of the past, AI is available to every company and individual. Adaptation by companies, people, and society is a structural feature of the technology itself and a challenge to safely manage.

Several experts opine on the existential threats to society, from the mass displacement of employees to the concentration of geopolitical power and the weaponization of AI. Contextually, this compares AI to nuclear technology. Like AI, there is a dual-use dilemma. Nuclear fission can be positive in electric energy production or negative in weapons. The same key technology unlocks both possibilities. Nuclear technology was an obvious danger after World War II, and governments, along with the UN, established atomic energy oversight. Governments exerted control over critical raw materials and production facilities. No company could privately use nuclear energy without consent. In contrast to the current AI industry, which is supported by a small number of companies with extraordinary investments in AI, those companies are racing to build technology on a scale that overshadows the Manhattan Project. The leadership of AI companies has a level of authority that surpasses governments.[3] It also means they have an equivalent obligation to their citizens that is rarely and inconsistently addressed.

■ ■ ■

The noise will never go away. It also will never be the same as it was in the past. The information environment described in this book is a permanent condition, not a crisis to be resolved, but a landscape to be navigated. Living in the noise is not a temporary state. It *is* simply where we live.

From my years in industry, as a researcher, and as an academic, I can sense that we are at an important moment. What has been surprising is not the manipulation itself, but the clarity with which the organizations behind it understand what they are doing. Platforms understand with analytic precision how their systems narrow our view, exploit the fault lines between our instinctive and deliberate thinking, and substitute engagement for truth. How they enable others to do so, how they permit that to exist. They have known this for years. Employees and whistleblowers have stepped forward. Congressional testimony. The voices of investigative journalists and those of concerned parents. The platforms continue anyway, displacing the journalists and governments they are quietly replacing without accepting the responsibility those institutions carry. Our urgency is not to react to the current version of AI. It is to collectively shape its future.

AI is inescapable, and when described that way, you might think it means you need to submit to a version of the future that those using AI have designed. It is quite the opposite. AI can make the world extraordinary. AI can make *you* extraordinary. How we decide to live with it, with acceptance or resistance, is not a small decision, even when it feels like one.

Somewhere tonight an engineer who helped build one of these systems is scrolling through a feed that she knows better than to trust because she helped design it. She is doing what you are doing. Living in the noise, looking for fragments that matter, scrolling past those that don't. That search, which is uncertain, imperfect, yet remains stubbornly human, is where truth lives.

Notes

1. Some studies indicate that people spend about 4 hours per day on social media, with younger people spending more time.
   Seydi Ahmet Satici, Ece Gocet Tekin, Mehmet Engin Deniz, and Burak Satici, "Doomscrolling Scale: Its Association with Personality Traits, Psychological Distress, Social Media Use, and Wellbeing," *Applied Research in Quality of Life* 18, no. 2 (2023): 833–847, `https://doi.org/10.1007/s11482-022-10110-7`
2. Octopuses' ability to think has long been underestimated. Researchers have demonstrated how they can solve puzzles, lift enclosure lids, and unscrew jars. They have the ability to survive outside of water for up to an hour and have demonstrated memories of previous events. Several reports show aquarium owners, from novice to professionals, discounting the ability of these creatures to problem-solve. Most famously, an octopus at the National Aquarium of New Zealand named Inky left its tank behind, crawled across the floor, and down a drain toward the ocean.
   Dan Bilefsky, "Inky the Octopus Escapes From a New Zealand Aquarium," *The New York Times*, April 13, 2016, `www.nytimes.com/2016/04/14/world/asia/inky-octopus-new-zealand-aquarium.html`
3. Investment in AI is historically extraordinary. The United States' nuclear weapons program, the Manhattan Project, cost $1.9 billion in 1945, the equivalent of $36 billion today. AI companies are expected to spend $650 billion in 2026 alone, an increase over the $400 billion spent in 2025. Most of the investments are in data centers; however, the development of OpenAI's ChatGPT has a cumulative cost of $180 billion.
   Nestor Maslej, Loredana Fattorini, Raymond Perrault, et al., *The 2025 AI Index Report* (Stanford, CA: Institute for Human-Centered Artificial Intelligence, Stanford University, 2025), `https://hai.stanford.edu/ai-index/2025-ai-index-report`

Acknowledgments

Books about complicated topics are rarely written alone, and I would be remiss to close out these pages without acknowledging those who made this book possible.

At Wiley, Lindsey Givens deserves credit for encouraging this idea that I couldn't shake about the impact of AI on society and how it was a worthy topic for a book. She also introduced me to Pete Gaughan, who became my managing editor. When we first met, he said there was not a technology topic that he couldn't handle. His years of work on technology books while based in San Francisco and Silicon Valley did not disappoint. He helped keep me on topic and on task, and I am grateful for the care that both have brought to this project.

Jeff Camm is the kind of colleague every writer should have to help you think more clearly. Our collaboration on *Data Duped* sharpened the ideas that eventually became this book, and his friendship has been constant throughout. I am thankful for that lunch where we realized there was purpose in writing a book about data deception. Wake Forest University and my work with analytics students were as much an education for me as they were for the students. Their questions fostered new ideas and research that were invaluable. Every professional should be as fortunate as to have the opportunity to work both in the classroom and in the corporate world and to appreciate what each has to offer and how one can benefit the other.

Thousands of words are written. Thousands of ideas are tossed away. What remains, hopefully, are those that matter, that speak to a reader, that eventually have a voice of their own. Many of my friends (too many to name them all) throughout the years have been my sounding board. A project meeting, a lunch conversation, even a quick hallway chat, all have shaped the topics of my writing. I write for them and hope that where I do not provide answers, I at least provide guidance. AI, like the technology that underpins it, is ever-changing and so are its solutions.

What is not ever-changing is the support I have from my family. My children and their futures are a constant reminder that I am writing for them as well. The moral and ethical dilemmas of AI are also a task for their generation. To my wife, Cristie, there are not enough words to describe the kind of support you have given me. From the adventures of our life to early discussions about what this book could really be about, your encouragement helped make this a better book.

I also want to acknowledge AI. You might be thinking that is an odd thing to do, because some of this writing is about the threat of AI. That's fair. But I also want readers to appreciate AI for what it can do, which is to help all of us be better. The point of the previous pages is to make sure it really does help us be better, that we use it wisely, and that those who are shaping how it works, consider those necessary guardrails.

This has been a human-written book. I know this will not be the last time in history a disclaimer like this is necessary. There will be, after all, more books written by AI, but I am hoping this is not the last one written by a human. The fact that these types of disclaimers are necessary is frankly a marker of where we are in the history of our society.

I used AI as a research assistant, and it was an invaluable time saver that helped me focus on the academic research that mattered and provided summaries where it was less important. Besides AI daily briefings, I also used it as an editor to provide recommendations and keep track of topics and the pace of my writing. Again, the efficiency of looking at the metrics of my narrative, like word counts and paragraph diagrams, is far beyond the capabilities of Microsoft Word just a few years ago. As an experiment, I also used AI to interview me for the About the Author section. Admittedly it was not perfect. It was a very long interview, and I needed to provide it with a lot of background information, but in the end, it worked out well after my final edits.

A team of people (and AI) helped put all this together, and I hope you enjoyed the collaboration as much as I did.

—dwg

About the Author

Derek W. Gibson spent more than two decades inside one of the largest financial institutions in America, watching how decisions actually get made. Not the decisions described in strategy decks or annual reports, but the real ones, built from incomplete data, shaped by assumptions nobody examined, and increasingly filtered through algorithms that nobody fully understood. His job, as Executive Director, VP of Analytics at Wells Fargo, was to make sense of the noise. It turned out to be good preparation for writing this book.

Gibson spent his career at the intersection of human behavior and data systems, building analytics capabilities across banking, retirement services, marketing, and client intelligence. He learned early that the most dangerous moment in any analysis is not when the data is wrong; it is when the data looks right but the question was never fully framed. That lesson, that the machinery of information can mislead even the people running it, became the animating idea behind everything he has written and taught since.

He is the coauthor, with Jeffrey D. Camm, the Inmar Presidential Chair at Wake Forest University's School of Business, of *Data Duped: How to Avoid Being Hoodwinked by Misinformation*, published by Rowman & Littlefield. The book, a practical guide to navigating deceptive data and flawed reasoning, established Gibson's voice in a conversation that has only grown louder with generative AI. *Data, AI, and Noise* picks up where that work left off and arrives somewhere more urgent. ChatGPT didn't invent misinformation; it industrialized it. And the companies doing the building, by and large, are still looking at what the technology can do next, not what it already has done.

But the more he looked, the clearer it became that personal defense alone is not enough. The platforms, the algorithms, the news ecosystem, and the governments meant to oversee them are all part of the problem, and any meaningful solution needs to demand something from them too.

Gibson is an adjunct professor in graduate programs and also serves on the advisory board of the Wake Forest University School of Business's Master of Science in Business Analytics program. He has spoken to corporate executives, military leaders, and academic audiences on AI strategy, misinformation, and the expanding gap between the data organizations collect and the decisions they actually need to make. His lectures do not settle for the abstract. They are built from the same real instinct that shaped his career:

That the most important thing you can do with a complex system is understand where it fails.

Gibson grew up in Maine and resides in North Carolina, close enough to the ocean to feel at home. As a lifelong sailor, he learned early to be curious and cautious of unpredictable seas—those in front of you and those on the horizon.

Index

A

A/B testing, 82, 184
aggregation, 125, 149
AI. *See* artificial intelligence (AI)
AIDS, 139
algorithms, 71–82, 84, 85, 116–117, 121, 123, 128, 129, 133, 135, 184, 185, 187, 189, 190, 193
  emotional algorithms, 67–68
AlphaFold, 161–162
AlphaGo Zero, 162
Alzheimer disease, 139, 190
America Online (AOL), 11
Amodei, Dario (Anthropic CEO), 190
amygdala hijacking, xiv
Andreu-Sánchez, Celia, 65
Andromeda model, 79
Anthropic, 92, 104, 105, 126, 166, 187, 188, 190–192
API, 110
Apple, 104, 160, 191
Aristotle, 31, 32
artificial intelligence (AI), x, xi, xii, xv, xvi, xvii, 1, 20, 21, 25, 29–32, 38–40, 43, 44, 48–51, 55–57, 62, 71, 84, 88, 91–93, 100, 104, 105, 117–118, 127, 129–131, 133–135, 183–196
  Action Summit, 167, 181
  vs AI tools, 108–111
  algorithms, 116–117
  Brussels Effect, 159–160, 168
  communication with others, 2–4
  detection, 111–113
  five stages, 113–116
  Impact Summit, 166–169
  marketing analysis, 125
  mechanisms, 79–82
  media landscape, 1–2
  power, 160–161

artificial intelligence (*continued*)
information environment, 164–165
infrastructure dependency, 162–164
labor globalization, 164
military applications, 165–166
scientific compression, 161–162
regulations, 170–176
Safety Institute, 167
Safety Summit, 166–169
self-regulation, 176–180
technology tools, 108–111
truth, 193
uses of attackers, 126
verification moment, 107–108
Asimov, Isaac, 191
Associated Press (AP), 25, 110
A. Tinker Tailor Soldier Spy, 147, 154
Augenstein, Isabelle, 158
AuthorMist, 109, 110

B

BASIC, 98
B. Dracula, 147
behavioral data, 74
behavioral model, 122
Bekos, Paschalis, 138
Bellingcat, 140–141, 152, 153
Berners-Lee, Tim, 12
Bernstein, Carl, 15
Bigfoot, 89, 90, 104
Bilefsky, Dan, 196
black-box models, 52, 81, 82, 140, 189, 190
Black Lives Matter movement, 16
Blake, Oli, 147, 153, 154
Bloomberg News, ix, x
bogus AI-generated research, 109
Borenstein, Nina, 158
Boston Marathon bombing, 154
Boston News-Letter, 7
Boston Times, 186
Branson, Richard, 104
Breaking News, 117, 174
broadcasting, 27
Brokaw, Tom, 11
Brookings Institution, 136
Brussels Effect, 159–160, 168
Buk missile system, 140, 141, 157
ByteDance, 68, 69

C

Cambridge Analytica–Facebook scandal, 84, 86, 161
Candler, Asa, 97
cargo transportation, 170
CBS Evening News, 11, 18

Center for AI Standards and Innovation (CAISI), 167
centralized sources, 142–147
CERN, 13
Charlotin, Damien, 119
ChatGPT, x, xi, 49, 56, 87, 104, 109, 113, 126, 159, 163, 164, 166, 188, 196, 202
Chesterfield King cigarettes, 17
Chicago Tribune, 11
Children's Online Privacy Protection Act (COPPA), 69
Cho, Haehyun, 137
Claude, xi, 104, 126, 188, 191
Cloud Cuckoo Land (Doerr), 4
Coalition for Content Provenance and Authenticity (C2PA), xiii
COBOL, 98
Coca-Cola, 72, 97, 98, 105
Cofacts, 152, 153
cognitive processing fluency, 54
coherence theory, 32, 34
collective intelligence, 154–155
Communications Decency Act of 1996, 102
community, 2, 3, 16, 72, 74, 80, 93, 98, 102, 123, 124, 141, 143–146, 151, 152, 155, 157, 169, 177, 178
computer-generated imagery (CGI), 38
consensus theory, 32–33
conspiracy theories, 38–39
Constitutional AI, 191
content-selection algorithms, 78
contextual data, 74
Conway, Kellyanne, 42
correspondence theory, 31, 33
Couric, Katie, 11
COVID-19 pandemic, 19
Crabtree, Edward, 174
Cronkite, Walter, 11
crowdsourced verification, 147–154
Cybersecurity Law, 69

D

Daily AUS, 174, 175
The Daily News, 23, 24, 27
DALL·E, xi, xii, xiii
D'Amelio, Charli, 99
DARPA, 12
data, xi, xiii, 14, 25–27, 29, 31, 42, 45, 48, 49, 58, 61, 67, 69–72, 75–79, 81, 84–86, 110, 111, 115, 121–125, 129, 131–134, 137, 142, 148, 160, 162–167, 177, 178, 184, 188–190, 196, 197
  ecosystem, 131–134

data (*continued*)
privacy, 124
professionals, 169, 189
types
behavioral data, 74
contextual data, 74
explicit data, 73–74
inferred data, 74
relational data, 74
third-party data, 74
Day, Benjamin Henry
The New York Sun, 8
decentralization process, 148–149
DeepMind, 112, 118
project, 161–162
DeepSeek, 113, 163, 168
Defense Advanced Research Projects Agency (DARPA), 12
Deloitte Center for Financial Services projects, 126
Democratic National Committee, 14
Deniz, Mehmet Engin, 196
Department of Health and Human Services, 172
De Waal, Kayle B., 45
Digital Services Act (DSA), 175
digital solidarity economy (DSE), 152
diversity, of knowledge, 148
Doerr, Anthony, 5
Cloud Cuckoo Land, 4
Döpke, Jörg, 120
Dove, 137
Duarte, Marcelo, 65
Dubinskiy, Sergey, 157

E

Easterbrook, Frank H. (Federal Judge), 172
Eaton, Misty J., 64
echo chamber effect, 36, 37, 44, 128–130, 135
Edinburgh Journal of Science (Herschel), 9
Elliott, Daniel, 158
emotional algorithms, 67–68
European Economic Area (EEA), 175
European Organization for Nuclear Research, 13
European Union AI Act, 159
explicit data, 73–74

F

Facebook, xiii, 16, 22, 30, 35–36, 52, 59, 65, 71–73, 78, 79, 81, 83, 84, 100, 114, 116, 118, 123, 128, 129, 133, 143, 145, 146, 150, 151

fact-checking approach, 144, 145, 150–153, 155, 157, 158
Fattorini, Loredana, 196
FBI, 154, 155
Federal Communications Commission (FCC), 18, 20, 25, 28, 30
Federal Trade Commission (FTC), 69, 85, 172, 173
Ferres, Juan Lavista, 65
Fiedler, Alexandra, 120
Flat Earth Society, 33, 35
Flight MH17, 139–141, 157
Foreign Adversary Controlled Applications Act, 69
Franklin, Benjamin, 6

G

Gemini, xi, 176, 188
GenAI. *See* generative AI
General Data Protection Regulation (GDPR), 159, 160, 171
generative AI (GenAI), ix, xi, xvi, 47, 49, 56, 63, 87, 90, 91, 96, 108, 109, 116–118, 120, 125, 126, 133, 143, 185, 189, 190
generative pre-trained transformers (GPTs) models, xi, 90, 96, 109–110
Gimlin, Robert, 89
Girkin, Igor, 157
Golubeva, Tatiana B., 64
Google effect, 59, 60
Goslin, Jeremy, 66
government/academic institutions, 14–15
GPTZero, 109, 110, 120
graphics processing units (GPUs), 47, 163
Grisham, John, 111
Grok, 153, 174, 175
Gutenberg, 6, AU: Please provide full name for "Gutenberg"

H

H800, 171
Harfort Courant, 7
Haugen, Frances, 80–81
Hearst, William Randolph, 105
Henry, Derrick, 100
Heo, Honyeong, 137
Herring, Clyde (Senator), 24
Herschel, Sir John, 9
Higgins, Eliot, 139–140
high-choice environments, 52
Hilbert, Martin, 62
Homer, 22
Iliad and *Odyssey,* 4
Hooper, C. E., 25–28
HTTPS, 172

Hugging Face Transformers library, 112
Humboldt Times, 89
Hypertext Transfer Protocol, 12–13

I

IBM, 97–98, 126, 159
ICANN, 175
Iliad (Homer), 4
illusory truth effect, 59
imitation game, 120
independence conditions, 148
Industrial Revolution, 8, 92, 194
inferred data, 74
Internet, xi, xvii, 11–13, 16–18, 35, 48, 49, 59, 60, 74, 118, 132, 146, 162, 172, 173, 176
Internet of Things (IoT), 161
Inyushin, Mikhail, 64
IRS, 143

J

jazz musician, 48
Jennings, Peter, 11
Jia, Lei, 65
Jiang, Yuwej, 65
Joint Investigation Team (JIT), 141
Jones Act, 170, 182

K

Kahneman, Daniel, 96
Keijzer, Karlijn, 139
Kennedy, John Fitzgerald Jr., 36, 51, 52, 55
Kharchenko, Leonid, 157
Kickstarter project, 141
King, Stephen, 111
Kleinman, Zoe, 181
"knowledge is power," 164
Korneeva, Elena, 64
Kourtellis, Nicolas, 138
Kubrick, Stanley, 38

L

Lange, Dr. Joep (AIDS researcher), 139
large language model (LLM), x, 159
lateral reading, 114, 117
Law of the Horse approach, 172, 173
Lerner, Alan Jay, 57, 66
Levy, Daniel, 105
Levy, Nekima, 131
liability, 177
libraries, 8, 112, 146
  as source of truth, 4–7
liquefied natural gas (LNG), 181, 182
Locke, Richard Adams, 9, 22
Los Angeles Times, 11, 127
Louvre, 146

M

Madison, James, 191
Mahara, Arpan, 120
Mahomes, Patrick, 100
Makarov, Vladimir I., 64
Manhattan Project, 179, 194, 196
marketing analysis, for generations, 125
Martín-Pascual, Miguel Ángel, 65
Marx, Chico, 49
Maslej, Nestor, 196
McEntire, Reba, 100
McMahon, Liv, 181
mental effect, 54
Meta Pixel, 137
Me Too movement, 16
Metsola, Roberta, 159
Microsoft, 30, 97, 98, 199
military innovations, 5
Misra, Amit, 65
MIT, 50
Mitchell, John, 15
monthly active authors (MAAs), 150
Moon Hoax, 9
MrBeast, 99
Murrow, Edward R., 11
Musical. ly, 68, 85
Musk, Elon, x, 146, 157

N

National Aquarium of New Zealand, 196
National Daily Journal, 186
National Intelligence Law, 69
National Park Service, 42
National Transportation Safety Board (NTSB), 99
natural-born instincts, 49–53
Nessie, 88–89
Neutral Point of View (NPOV), 150
New Jersey Journal, 7
Newman, Eryn J., 65
news influencers, 18, 19, 101
newspaper, 10–16, 18, 23–32, 35, 36, 43–45, 83, 90, 93, 94, 99, 101, 105, 117, 127, 128, 135, 144
  in United States, 7–9
Newsweek magazine, 130
The New York Journal, 93, 105
The New York Sun (Day), 8–10
The New York Times, 11, 13, 18, 23–25, 27, 45, 92, 94, 96, 101, 102, 146
The New York World, 93, 105
NFL, 100
Nixon, Richard, 15
noise, xvi, 20–21, 33, 44, 100, 112, 142, 155, 174, 186, 195

noise (*continued*)
information, 20–21
and judgment, 62–63
recognization, 94–95
nongovernmental organizations (NGOs), 153
nuclear fission, 194
nuclear technology, 194
NVIDIA, 163, 166, 168, 171

O

octopus, 188, 196
Odyssey (Homer), 4
OPEC, 163
OpenAI, x, xi, xiii, 49, 56, 92, 159, 163, 166, 171, 191, 196
Oppenheimer, J. Robert, 179
Opree, Suzanna J., 85
Orwell, George, 40–42
Outcault, Richard F., 105

P

Panoplai, 137
Papadopoulos, Panagiotis, 138
Patriot Press, 7
Patterson, Roger, 89
Pennsylvania Evening Post, 7
Pennsylvania Gazette, 7
Perrault, Raymond, 196
personal computer (PC), xi, xvii
personalization engines, 72–79
Pew Research Center, 13, 14, 19
pixels, 47, 112, 132, 133, 137
Plato, 31, 32, 108, 109
Poe, Edgar Allan, 10
POLES, 34
PolitiFact, 144, 153
Polychronakis, Michalis, 138
Post Office Act of 1792, 7
pragmatic theory, 32
"pro-growth AI policies," 181
Public Benefit Mission, 92
Pulitzer, Joseph, 105
Putin, Vladimir, 160–161
Python, 189, 190

R

Rather, Dan, 11
Reddit, 71, 73, 83, 129, 147, 154
relational data, 74
responsible artificial intelligence in the military domain (REAIM), 166
Rishe, Naphtali, 120
risk metrics, 178
Rober, Mark, 99
RoBERTa, 118
Roca, Thomas, 65
Roman, Anthony Cintron, 65
Rowbotham, Samuel Birley, 33
Russian Ministry of Defense, 141

S

sandboxes, 187
Satici, Burak, 196
Satici, Seydi Ahmet, 196
Savvinov, Alexey, 64
Sawyer, Diane, 11
Schilder, Cor, 139
Schwarz, Norbert, 65
Scientific Method, 31
Segijn, Claire M., 85
Serling, Rod, 17, 18
Sim, Kyungmin, 137
Simpson, O.J., 130
Skatchkov, Serguei N., 64
Smith, Winston, 40, 41
social media, xiii, xiv, xv, xvi, 17–19, 22, 26, 32, 35–38, 43, 51, 59, 68–73, 75, 77–79, 81–85, 90, 94, 95, 97, 99–102, 108, 115–117, 122, 123, 127–130, 132, 134, 140, 143, 144, 146, 150, 152–155, 158, 161, 176–178, 184, 187, 189, 192, 196
  influencers, 15–20
  photos purposes, 52–53
Societal Impacts Team, 191
Socrates, 160
SORA, 56
source criticism, 114
Stephenson, George, 92
Strycharz, Joanna, 85
Sumer region of Mesopotamia, 3
Surowiecki, James, 147
synthetic data generation, 133–134
SynthID, 112, 118

T

targeted algorithm workflow
  feedback, 77
  prediction, 76
  presentation, 77
  ranking, 76–77
  selection, 76
  signal, 75
  variety of content, 77
Tekin, Ece Gocet, 196
Television Code of 1952, 17, 18
thedailyaus.world, 174, 175
third-party data, 74, 124
Tian, Edward, 109
TikTok, 16, 68–70, 73, 76, 78, 80, 83, 89, 90, 100, 102, 116, 129, 146, 172
Time magazine, 130
The Times of London, 10
Tol, Neeltje, 139
Torre, Ilaria, 66
TRESemmé, 137
Tripathi, Sunil, 154

truth, xvi, 14, 18, 19, 21, 28–31, 34, 36–40, 63, 71, 78, 82, 83, 93, 95, 96, 99, 101, 102, 108, 110, 121, 131, 139, 141, 142, 144, 145, 150, 155, 169, 175, 189
alternative facts, 40–43
coherence theory, 32
consensus theory, 32–33
correspondence theory, 31
event, 192–195
illusory truth effect, 59
libraries as source, 4–7
negotiating, 43–44
newspapers, 23–26
pragmatic theory, 32
referee, 29–30
truth-and accuracy-gatekeeping function, 87–90
truthiness effect, 53–55
truth-and accuracy-gatekeeping function, 87–90
truthiness effect, 54, 55
Turing, Alan, 120
Turing test, 110
Turner, Anna, 85
The Twilight Zone, 17
Twitter, 16, 22, 73, 76, 83, 85, 86, 88, 90, 102, 114, 129, 131, 145, 146, 150–153, 155, 157, 175, x, xi, xiii, xv

U
UN Declaration of Human Rights, 191
UNESCO survey (2024), 20
United Nations Technology and Innovation Report, 165
United States Department of Defense, 12
United States Department of Justice, 15
United States, newspaper in, 7–9
UPS, 98–100

V
van Gogh, Vincent, 47
van Tongeren, Jacqueline, 139
Vega, Jehú Torres, 65
Velásquez-Salamanca, Daniela, 65
Vietnam War, 14

W
The Wall Street Journal, xiv, 11, 79–81, 83, 127
Wang, Pengce, 65
Wang, Qi, 59
The War of the Worlds, 23–28, 43, 44
Warren, George, 158
Washington, George, 7
The Washington Post, 11, 15, 145

The Washington Register, 186
Watergate scandal, 14, 37
watermarks, xii, xiii
Welles, Orson, 23, 26, 27
Wells, H. G., 23
White, Kevin, 65
White, Laurence, 66
Wikipedia, 147, 149–153
Wilson, Robert Kenneth, 88, 104
window dressing, 53, 56
WinstonAI, 109, 110
Woodward, Bob, 15
World Economic Forum, 169, 192, 193
World Health Organization, 146
World War I, 170
World War II, 10, 11, 37, 104, 194
World Wide Web, 12

X

X/Twitter. *See* Twitter

Y

Yang, Luyu, 68
Yang, Xiaojing, 65
Young, Andrew, 105

Z

Zayas-Santiago, Astrid, 64
Zhu, Alex, 68
Zuckerberg, Mark, 146, 157
Zueva, Lidia V, 64